DREAM GARAGES

KRIS PALMER

Foreword by Peter Egan

motorbooks

For my parents, Karl and Marilyn Palmer

ACKNOWLEDGMENTS

This book exists because a lot of interesting, talented, and generous people shared their time, skills, knowledge, and remarkable collections. To all of the garage owners—thanks for your kind generosity in opening your doors and sharing your amazing collections of cars, bikes, trucks, memorabilia, and art. Every fan of the motorized world benefits from having these treasures preserved, especially by owners who care and know so much about them. Because garages and automobilia are visual wonders that must be seen to be appreciated, thanks to photographers Peter Vincent, Robert Genat, James Mann, Peter Martin, and David Gooley for snapping a lot of great pictures. A few of us can enjoy a vehicle itself, but we can all admire lines and details captured in a photograph. At Motorbooks, Zack Miller, Lee Klancher, Erica Kritsberg, and many unsung heroes turn ideas and word-processing files into appealing, enduring books that can reach many readers. It's an honor to be involved in that process. Thanks, too, to Ann Mulaney for sharing her skills in Italian, Theresa Lippert for sending me to her, the late Genevieve Obert for her interviews and information about the Righini collection, and my wife, Jenneane, for putting up with me and all my projects.

First published in 2006 by Motorbooks, an imprint of MBI Publishing Company, 400 First Avenue North, Suite 300, Minneapolis, MN 55401 USA

© 2012 Motorbooks
Text © 2012 Kris Palmer

Motorbooks titles are also available at discounts in bulk quantity for industrial or sales-promotional use. For details write to Special Sales Manager at MBI Publishing Company, 400 First Avenue North, Suite 300, Minneapolis, MN 55401 USA.

To find out more about our books, visit us online at www.motorbooks.com.

ISBN-13: 978-0-7603-4339-5

Printed in China

Editor: Zack Miller
Design Manager: Cindy Samargia Laun
Designers: Tom Heffron and Jennifer Maass

On the cover:
Bill Goldberg's Mopar muscle shrine. *Robert Genat*

On the frontispiece:
Tools and inspiration in Steve Hamel's garage. *Peter Martin*

On the title pages:
Mark Morton's garagemahal shines in the California dusk. *Robert Genat*

On the back cover:
(Top) John Shirley's cars are beautifully presented, but they're also driven regularly and with gusto. *David Gooley*
(Lower) Ron Jolliffe's Rocket Science Engineering earns its name on the salt flats of Bonneville. *Peter Vincent*

A PARTICULAR FASCINATION

For a few people—the lucky ones, some might say—one thing above all others captures their imagination and becomes the central focus of their lives.

"Now where was I?" Believe it or not, this '67 E-type actually got reassembled and back on the road in less than two years. Or so.

As I write this, spring is arriving, and our last winter heating bill for my workshop just arrived in the mail yesterday. It's enough to make you bleed from the ear, and Barb has been shaking her head over the high cost of my hobby, wishing, no doubt, I'd take up bee-keeping or fly-tying or some pastoral diversion that doesn't require a separate building the size of our house.

But if she thinks I'm going to cease and desist anytime soon, she's out of luck. We may eventually move to a more sensible climate as we near retirement, but I'm into this large workshop mode for the duration.

This garage, you see, is more than just a place to work on cars and motorcycles. It has several other important social and psychological functions as well. It also serves as:

A museum of mechanical design. Many nights I go out to the garage not to work, but to sit with a cup of coffee or (ideally) a margarita and just *look* at my bikes and cars. To admire the lovely engine cases on my Triumph 650, the P-38-inspired twin-boom tail fins of my Harley Earl–designed Cadillac, or the neat, just-right envelope body of the Lotus Elan. Often, I move these things around and reposition them for better viewing. I call this "garage ikebana," after the Japanese art of landscape arrangement. Sometimes, I fix myself a second drink, and sit there into the wee hours, mesmerized. A warm electrical current of sheer pleasure surges through my brain with a near-audible hum. No art museum was ever this good.

A monastery. More and more often, I find the garage a perfect refuge from everything trashy in modern culture. It's an escape from bad television, news magazines filled with trivia, heartbreaking newspaper headlines, crime, government folly, war, bad music, and televised auto racing that's so commercial and contrived as to be unrecognizable for its original intent. You can retire to your garage, put a Miles Davis or Muddy Waters CD on your fabulous $25 garage-sale stereo system, turn your attention to the restoration of an old MG and make the world go away. Everything crass and second-rate fades into the distance. It's the inner sanctum, the private chapel inside your castle walls. I've considered putting stained glass windows in my shop, with Colin Chapman depicted as one of the 12 disciples, but that may be going too far.

A clubhouse. If you're like me—and who isn't?—your family probably doesn't want you putting up Steve McQueen *Great Escape* posters on your living room wall, or tin signs that advertise Castrol R and Vincent Motorcycles. They probably don't want eighth-place racing trophies, bent connecting rods or Jaguar knock-offs on the fireplace mantel, either. This stuff has all got to go someplace, so it goes in your garage. Then other people just like you start showing up and drinking beer, or hanging around to admire these fine posters and artifacts during car and motorcycle club meetings. You could hold these meetings at a public bar, but then you'd risk mingling with people who watch golf on TV. It's better to have your own place.

Sometimes, when I go out to the workshop and turn on the lights, I stand there for a moment and wonder whether the cars I'm restoring matter as much to me as the place where I work on them. It's reciprocal, I've decided. They bestow their magic on one another, combining to form the perfect refuge. With heat and compressed air.

Peter Egan

Your garage is the perfect place to make noises that no one else wants to hear. Except for the other guys in your garage band, who seem not to care. *Photo by Brian Blades/ Road & Track Magazine*

For instance, it's impossible to decide if your MGB really needs its points adjusted when your feet are frozen, or to rebuild a transmission when your tools feel like they've been dipped in liquid oxygen.

Also, if it's cold enough to see your breath, it's probably too cold to use a can of spray paint. The little ball bearing sounds like someone with a pipe wrench trapped in a submarine. And your air compressor groans when it tries to start, and all the lights go dim, and . . . well . . . I won't belabor the point. Essentially heat is good; cold is bad. A real workshop needs to be a warm and inviting place.

So we moved to Wisconsin and found a nice old mill house (with the mill missing) on 16 acres, with a 2 1/2-car garage to hold our "regular" daily cars and lawn equipment. And about 15 minutes after we moved the last stick of furniture into the house, I called a contractor to begin work on my dream garage. After a lifetime of putting up with miserable little attached one- or two-car garages that had to hold lawnmowers, potting soil, laundry appliances, Weber grills, and old bicycles—in addition to our cars, of course—I was determined to have something better.

Considering that I designed the workshop myself with a piece of graph paper and a crayon, it didn't turn out too bad. It ended up as a 30-by-40-foot heated workshop with windows and skylights and a Kentucky-cabin type porch. I installed (finally!) a really huge two-stage upright air compressor that can actually run air tools and a bead blasting cabinet—without jittering across the floor. I also built in some big workbenches and a small Japanese refrigerator to hold beer.

It took about four months to build the place (when roofers say they'll be back on Monday, they don't necessarily mean any Monday in your own lifetime), but they finally got it done, just before the first snowfall. We had a big garage-warming party with free beer and food, and I turned the heat on. It blew down upon us like rays from a benevolent sun.

There's an LP gas furnace suspended from the ceiling in one corner, with heat ducting that runs the length of the shop and blows warm air, almost instantly, in all directions. I leave it set at 50 degrees in the winter, and when I go out there to work at night I kick it up to 65 or 70. Within five minutes I can be working in a T-shirt. This may be a rather large carbon footprint for a person of my modest mechanical skills to be leaving on this earth, but I defend it as the cost of being alive and moderately happy.

I'm a serial restorer of old cars and bikes, so in the past 16 years this shop has witnessed the resuscitation of an MGB, Porsche 356, Jaguar E-type, two old Cadillacs and (current project) a Lotus Elan, not to mention four motorcycles and three Formula Ford racing cars. Right now, the shop is a little crowded, with three cars and four bikes in it.

Not to mention an entire carpeted corner for our garage band.

Yes, I'm a guitar player in a painfully loud blues band called the Defenders, and we have a permanent "sound stage" with drums, amps, and a huge sound system to emphasize our general ineptitude. Unfortunately, the band area occupies enough space to hold at least one more 1953 Cadillac Fleetwood, but then I don't really need another one. Actually, no one does.

Anyway, as *R&T* Editor Tom Bryant has pointed out, "If you're going to have a garage band, you need a garage. No one wants to hear a 'bathroom band' or a 'kitchen band.' It just isn't right."

There are costs, of course.

Foreword

The Inner Sanctum, with Heat and Compressed Air

When I talked my poor wife Barbara into moving back to Wisconsin from Southern California 16 years ago, she set down two nonnegotiable conditions:

"One: We will have a garage for my car so I don't have to shovel it out of a snow bank or scrape the windshield every morning. Two: I'll turn up the heat in our house as high as it takes to make me feel warm."

I could hardly argue, as half the reason I wanted to move back to the Midwest was to have enough land to build a great big workshop—with heat.

I can't remember what the other half was, but I think it involved eating bratwurst at Elkhart Lake.

In any case, my requirements for moving back to the frozen tundra pretty much paralleled Barb's. Getting your cars and motorcycles out of the weather in Wisconsin is almost a requirement of life itself, and being warm enough to think straight is an important component of mental balance. A shivering person is not a rational person.

When you've foolishly taken the entire front end off a Jaguar and the rear end off a race car, it's always good to have a few reliable old motorcycles that don't need any work. Or just sit back and have a beer.

Introduction

If this book is in your hands, you either love automobiles or motorcycles or care about someone who does. Their beauty, style, utility, speed, ability to move us physically and emotionally, have made them central to our existence since they displaced horses a century ago. Cars and bikes and the men and women who collect, ride, build, and restore them have changed the way we live in and look at the world.

But these vehicles do not just give. They also take. And the one thing all of them take is space. Whether built or bought for pleasure, speed, or utility, the vehicles we own need to go somewhere. That place is the garage. No matter how big your dreams or budget, if there's no place to put it, it has to go—or it can't come home in the first place. Wonderful machines have traded hands for no better reason than their owners had no place to keep them.

Garages are more than shelters, though. They are also a world unto themselves, where wonderful, mobile creations rest, recover, and take shape. Work in a garage is different from work at a desk, on the phone, in a suit, where grease and oil are the last things you want to encounter. In the garage, these lubricants are lifeblood and their presence is essential, their absence alarming. Pulling on some jeans or coveralls and heading into the garage is, for millions of enthusiasts, the work that's play—the reward at the end of a long week. Where our labors elsewhere produce a paycheck, our efforts in the garage make dingy metal gleam, scattered parts reconstitute, and pistons and gears once idle roar to life. That alone brings peace and satisfaction. Taking these machines out on the roads or tracks or dead-level salt at Bonneville offers thrills and pleasures like no others in life—our garage's greatest reward.

Dream Garages looks at 21 spaces filled with noteworthy cars, trucks, bikes, and related art and memorabilia. Some have a museum-like quality in their beauty, cleanliness, order. Others are working garages, where their owners create and tune machines that look or move like nothing else on wheels. Still others are eclectic collections—not spotless, but no less places where any of us would love to spend an afternoon studying the vehicles and objects on hand and hearing the stories behind them. Common to all of them is their owners' love and respect for motor vehicles and a desire to see them preserved—and used. This is not a study of particular types of collections, but a celebration of the auto enthusiast's favorite space—his treasure trove, his refuge, his place of peace.

The garages and collections in this book reach from California to Italy and include many unique and extraordinary vehicles and spaces. Their owners hold ribbons from Pebble Beach and land speed records at Bonneville. They are builders and drivers of hot rods; muscle cars; woodies; Jaguar, Ferrari, Alfa Romeo, and Group C sports cars; Vincent motorcycles; movie vehicles and rugged machines from World War II. Some of the most famous race car drivers in the world, including Michael Schumacher and Derek Bell, have driven cars in these collections, as have movie stars such as Johnny Depp and Jack Nicholson, and director Roberto Rosselini. Some of the best known fabricators, painters, upholsterers, and engine builders have worked on these wonderful rides.

Enthusiasts will also recognize the names on these photographs—top automotive snappers like Peter Vincent, James Mann, Robert Genat, and David Gooley spent a lot of time—and filled a lot of film and disc space—recording these provocative collections. Seeing is believing.

Each of these garage profiles is about the same length—just about right to read through at the end of a long day to drive off the hassles and renew your desire to get back into your own garage and turn a wrench or an ignition key. There are over 200 photos here and hundreds more exciting cars and bikes. We hope you enjoy looking at and learning about them as much as we have enjoyed bringing them to you.

—Kris Palmer

Contents

Nick Alexander

IRON MOUNTAIN MAGIC—FORD & MERCURY WOODIES

The warehouse in which Nick Alexander houses his Ford and Mercury woodie collection was built about the same time as the factory in Michigan where Henry Ford blended mechanical acumen and fine woodworking skill. *Robert Genat*

In the early days of the American automobile industry, in a place called Iron Mountain on Michigan's Upper Peninsula, Henry Ford acquired several hundred thousand acres of virgin timberland. Initially, that woodland provided various components for Model Ts and Model As. For 1932, Ford outfitted a station wagon with a wooden body, making frames out of Iron Mountain maple and birch. Other manufacturers built woodies too, but according to collector Nick Alexander, Ford's wood was the highest quality in the industry, featuring large pieces free of sapwood, knots, and other imperfections.

When Alexander was a child in Southern California, woodies were everywhere—motorized workhorses hauling people and goods. They form some of his earliest memories. His grandmother once inquired why this four-year-old was able to call out the manufacturers' names of cars his family passed on the road. No wonder Alexander's feet carried him into an auto dealership when he was ready for a job. The local Ford dealer hired him at age 14 or 15 as a "get-ready boy" to spiff up the cars. He befriended the used car manager, who would call him whenever something cheap came in that might interest Alexander. "I bought a lot of old cars," he says, but not to keep. Money was tight then.

Though he found his way to German luxury cars, selling BMWs in Southern California, Alexander never forgot the wood-bodied wagons of his youth. In 1994 that interest returned. Big time. That was the year he bought his first collectible woodie—it only fueled the fire. He loved the car, and it inspired him to set an

There isn't a bad side on a woodie wagon—the paneled tailgate and color-matched spare tire holder show an attention to detail all but lost in modern production cars. Overhead, you could hardly ask for more windows to keep the space airy and well lit. *Robert Genat*

A 1946 Ford Sportsman body awaiting trim.

This one speaks for itself. Just what got done at Iron Mountain gets done here (or more accurately, at the shop up the street). *Robert Genat*

incredible goal: to collect one example of every wood-bodied Ford and Mercury wagon from the flathead era, 1932 to 1953.

If the streets of his youth were well populated with woodies, those near the turn of the millennium were not. Most were gone forever; those that remained were distributed among the rest of the nation's old cars—in private collections, moldering junkyards, quiet barns, and the occasional field open to the elements' ravages. Rough examples were outside Alexander's quest. He sought the best cars, complete and proper vehicles capable of being restored to pristine condition—or far rarer, cars so well preserved that restoration would only detract from their charm.

His hunt for the wood-bodied grail has taken Alexander all over the country. "I've seen areas where my only reason to go was to chase a car," he says. Sometimes it's a bust—the car isn't what the owner said it was. But as Alexander points out, "The good stories make up for the wild goose chases."

One lead took him across the country, to Captainsville, New Hampshire. Alexander chased down a name he found in a roster of old car owners. He rang the man, and they had a great conversation. The car was a '42 Merc, still running and fondly cared for. The man had used it to take his kids to summer camp most recently, and it had only been a few years since he had driven it. Alexander hopped a flight, rented a car, found Captainsville, and hunted down the man's farm.

What he found was a surprise. The man was advanced in years, and there were no kids around. They went back to the barn, where the Merc lay beneath a tarp. At least it might have been a

Alexander's ambitious quest, begun in the mid-1990s, was to acquire an outstanding example of every Ford and Mercury woodie from the flathead era. He has finally achieved that goal. Most of the cars have been restored to pristine condition; a few were so outstanding when he got them that they were too good to restore. *Robert Genat*

This is a genuine firebox from Ford's woodie plant in Iron Mountain, Michigan. Alexander has visited the area and met the son of a man who worked in the factory. He'd love to find some original tooling, but he fears most of it was scrapped. *Robert Genat*

Merc. It was hard to see, because years of bric-a-brac were piled on top of it—more than a couple of years. Alexander and the farmer spent half an hour relocating items so that they could uncover the car. It had last been licensed in 1955.

The car was complete though, and a year Alexander did not yet own. If the man had misled him, it was not intentional. "I'd really like to buy it," Alexander told him. "Oh, I thought you just wanted to see it," the farmer replied. "I couldn't sell it. This is the car I took my kids to camp in." Goose chase, it seemed. But the man had a suggestion: "Give me your name and number, and I'll give it to my attorney. When I die, he can call you, and you can buy it."

The enlarged photos of the Iron Mountain plant, sourced from Ford's archives, add a very nice touch to this warehouse garage. The photos show workers in the original factory building the cars Alexander now collects and restores. *Robert Genat*

Gluing up shaped, mortised and tenoned maple or birch in a layout jig to form a rear door frame.

Nick Alexander has studied these cars about as much as anyone. And he'll go on doing it, because it's not just his business, it's what he loves. *Robert Genat*

This decal remains on an unrestored 1937 Ford. Though its story has been lost, it may show support for U.S. involvement in World War II. After the Nazis torpedoed but did not sink the USS *Kearny*, President Franklin D. Roosevelt said in a speech: "Damn the torpedoes; full speed ahead!" *Robert Genat*

Alexander never heard from the attorney, yet the Captainsville Merc was not lost. It did come available, without Alexander's hearing about it, and a friend of his from the East Coast snapped it up. He was unwilling to sell the find, but he did ask Alexander if he would restore it. Fair enough; if he couldn't

This 1934 Ford station wagon has a simple elegance and design harmony, with the hood louvers complementing the grille's fine vertical bars and the wood panels' vertical frame members. The adjacent 1935 model connects the same elements with horizontal cues. The '34's side-mounted spare frees up additional space inside. *Robert Genat*

own this grail, he could at least bring the metal, paint, upholstery, and wood back to its former glory.

Today, Alexander has met his goal. He has about 50 Ford and Mercury woodies, most of which he has restored. A few of the vehicles are quite rare. He has two Marmon-Herrington four-wheel-drive woodies and knows of only a handful of others. His rarest is a 1946 Mercury Sportsman, of which only 205 were built. Alexander has never seen another, nor proof of one. Another rarity is a '41 Ford produced in Canada for military use. It was supposedly made for shipment to England or North Africa as a staff car, but it never left the country. It has special axles and tires for challenging terrain, and a desk that folds down from the back of the front seat—the idea being that an officer could sit in the back and plan a battle on the desk as he traveled.

The space housing the collection could hardly be more ideal. The cars fit comfortably side-by-side in two neat rows, illuminated by windows running the length of the walls below the ceiling. The building sits in an old industrial section of Los Angeles that was built about the same time as Henry Ford's factory in Iron Mountain. Alexander's restoration facilities lie just a short way up the road. He even has a fire alarm from the original woodie factory on the wall—a gift he received when he visited Iron Mountain to learn more about the town and the history of Ford's operations in the area.

The Marmon-Herrington all-wheel-drive models are also quite rare, with just a few known to exist. Alexander's shop restored this one, and most of the cars in the collection. *Robert Genat*

For anyone who visited a Ford dealership when these cars were new, they must resemble originals lined up for sale. But Alexander doesn't sell from his collection, except in a few cases when an even better example of a particular year has come along. Apart from that, these cars are to hold and to cherish—and also to drive. He puts a two-speed rear end, which works like overdrive, in all his cars for that purpose. "They're really reliable," he says. "People knock flatheads, but they're very roadworthy." He attributes the problems some people cite, like overheating, to cars that have not been well restored or maintained—cars with rust in the cooling systems, bad wiring, or other faults that don't haunt vehicles, once they're corrected. Alexander has driven woodies as far as Michigan and back with only pleasant miles to report.

The 1942 Mercury woodie is very rare, with fewer than 10 known examples remaining. An interesting design feature here, not unique to the '42, is the location of the turn signals, close to the center of the car. *Robert Genat*

This shot provides good perspective on similarities and differences between the two Ford Motor Company products. The windshield and surrounding sheet metal on this '49 Ford and '50 Mercury are very similar, while grille styles vary considerably. The raised portion of the newer Mercury's hood tapers more, which gives that aspect a slightly older look than the Ford. *Robert Genat*

On first encounter, the metal fenders and wooden panels seem a curious mix, but it takes only a minute to appreciate the care and craftsmanship that went into these vehicles. Henry Ford had his own forest for harvesting this wood, which Alexander says was of the highest standards in the industry. *Robert Genat*

At his restoration shop, Alexander handles the business side. "I'm a terrible mechanic," he laughs. "My job is to scour the U.S. and find the cars." He got into the restoration business because he was able to convince experts in the field to join him in his passion. "We have our own wood shop, mechanics, upholstery, and body shop"—and virtually no turnover. His employees love and respect these cars as much as he does.

In recent years, the collector hobby has found his passion too, and woodie prices are on the rise. This has made the cars a lot more expensive to buy; on the other hand, his collection is rising in value, too. That doesn't matter much to Alexander, though, because he has no plans to part with these treasures. He's still on the lookout for good cars, and he finds plenty of enjoyment bringing other people's wood-bodied wagons back to day-one condition.

Neil Tuckett

TUCKETT BROTHERS, EUROPE'S BIGGEST MODEL T SPECIALIST

Tuckett's daughters wanted to create an old-car centerpiece for the family's agricultural stand at a local show. Tuckett gestured to the parts piles and told them to build it themselves. The puzzle car was their creation, filled with flowers. *James Mann*

Some careers must be hunted like prey, across mountains and rivers, deserts and plains. Others show up at your door. Neil Tuckett did not enter the working world determined to become Europe's biggest Model T specialist. His great-uncle introduced the idea—though in nascent form. His particular proposal, made in 1978, was that he and Tuckett take a Model T on the London-to-Brighton run.

It's not old enough, Tuckett told him, since that event is for vehicles made before 1905. But the uncle persisted. He meant the London-to-Brighton commercial run. He had the truck, too—a 1924 one-ton van. In fact, he'd had it since the 1920s, when its cutting-edge capabilities doubled his family's sausages and pies business shuttling between their rural butcher shop and London. All the great-uncle and Tuckett needed was for Tuckett to get it running.

Tuckett had an agricultural engineering business, and Model Ts, like almost all the early cars and trucks, are pretty close to farm machines in their simplicity. Tuckett revived the old truck, and they made the proposed run—and had a great time. A short while later, the Model T knocked on his door again, sort

What year is it? Around the Tuckett Brothers garage, time is a little vague. It's always today, but ideas and machines and stories from across the decades meld present and past. There's a lot of history here. The "Ferguson" truck (1924) and the "Chertsey" truck (1925) are both one-ton Fords. *James Mann*

This sign is as accurate today as it was when some early Model T vendor first hung it on a wall—especially since vehicles that first passed beneath it may do so again here, the better part of a century later. *James Mann*

of. A friend who owned one wanted Tuckett to put valves in it. The future specialist accepted the repair opportunity, and did it well.

In 1981, just before Christmas, Tuckett and his brother bought a Model T Landaulette. They drove it home in the snow, which was a bit harrowing, and kept it for many years. Then in the early 1990s, the farming industry hit lean times. Tuckett found himself with a dozen employees and nothing for them to do.

But there was this fondness he had for the Ford Model T, a car his men could easily work on. There were not many Model Ts in England—yet there was not much competition repairing them, either. Besides, there will always be car collectors who fancy the spindly, indomitable little vehicle that got this whole automobile thing going on a grand scale in the first place.

If you're looking for Model T parts, Neil Tuckett's got a few around. He can even move among them without getting covered in grease, which puts him ahead of a lot of us—and probably rates well with wife, Mary, when he comes home from the shop. *James Mann*

Even in a car as basic as the Model T, there was variety for the car-hungry public. The spoked wheels are comparable on these three examples, but the four-passenger coachwork with fold-down top is a much different look from an open two-seater with windshield for one. *James Mann*

This is not an artistic rendition of the atom. It's a Model T made with two front ends, and two steering wheels. The car came from the United States, where it was supposedly built in 1929 for parades. *James Mann*

Tuckett dug in, gathering Model T cars, trucks, literature, repairs, hulks, and spares, and set up shop under the name Tuckett Brothers. A few of the Fords he's kept for himself, including the great-uncle's commercial van that indirectly kicked off this venture, or adventure. He's found some remarkable vehicles too, some remarkable for their features or history, others for a willingness to start and run after decades—better than half a century—of quiet neglect. But he isn't a man who can't let them go. Model Ts are his business, as well as his passion, so vehicles move in and out, some repaired for owners, others bought and sold to pay for a new day with an old invention.

One likely to stay is the Golden Ford, which Tuckett bought in 1983. At the time, he didn't realize he'd bought it. It was among a load of Model T stuff he acquired from an Englishman who'd been restoring the cars since the 1960s. What put Tuckett onto the car's heritage was its registration plate, which in England tends to stay with the car for life, unlike the United States, where license plates change with time or new owners. It meant nothing to him at first, but later, when he was thumbing through a book, Tuckett saw the same plate. It was affixed to an old race car with a golden body—a winning car raced at the famous Brooklands course from 1911 to 1914. The golden body was gone, the reason the car's past lay undetected, but most of the underlying car was there.

Britain's Channel 4 took interest in the car and produced a segment for its *Salvage Squad* program on the Golden Ford's restoration. Using old photographs, famed panel beater Rod

Tires, wheels, and inner tubes. If it's good, it stays, to be sold or put into a project. Among the parts and cars he buys, Tuckett also encounters old signs from the days when many people were in the business of selling and repairing Model Ts. *James Mann*

Model T engines were adapted for many uses. This cricket-pitch roller, used to flatten the playing area, was built around 1923. It's one of the Ford items that keep finding their way back to Tuckett. He's purchased and sold it on about five separate occasions. *James Mann*

Jolley painstakingly reconstructed the golden body down to the last rivet, with guidance from Tuckett and TV presenters Claire Barratt and Graham McPherson. (Fans of 1980s music may know McPherson as "Suggs," singer for the ska band, Madness.) The show revealed the car's story. The single-seat body wasn't actual gold, but brass. It was built by an early English Ford dealer and aviator, A. E. George, who wanted to race and also to make a statement. Tuckett believes the car was also raced after the Great War, around 1918: the engine was fitted with an overhead-valve conversion, which was not available during its Brooklands wins. It probably was no longer competitive by then, however.

Research into the car's history led to another surprise: George's daughter. She was 92 years old and willing to take part in the program. She met Tuckett and crew at Brooklands, where

There's a lot to be said for simple machines when you're the one doing the work. The car to the right came in for a starter-motor conversion. Imagine how long it would take to tear a modern car down to that level—and then get it back together. *James Mann*

Early Model Ts used sidelamps and taillamps powered with oil, typically kerosene (called paraffin in the U.K.). It's one of the components that closely ties the first Fords with their horse-drawn predecessors. *James Mann*

the car was reunited with the track. If there were any concerns over her age, she quickly dispelled them. "She was sharp as a whip," Tuckett says. She walked across Brooklands paddock to Tuckett and queried, "Young man, where did you get that body from?" It had been removed for her sister, she said, who was learning to drive and was too timid to take on the task in a one-seater car. The brass body sat in the family's workshop for years. Its final fate is unknown, though Tuckett thinks it was probably scrapped.

Another keeper is Rusty, named appropriately. "There's not a stitch of paint on it," Tuckett explains. That's part of this car's appeal. A circus family bought it in 1928, when the car was a year old. It went to the circus owner, who put it in a shed in 1931. The next time it

This customer car, with an overhead valve engine, was an American entry in the Great Race (a vintage car rally crossing the United States) in 1991, though the car resides in the U.K. The wheels have a period look but are modern items that Tuckett says must have come from "a very, very good facility" for pressing steel. *James Mann*

Steering wheels store easily, but the exacting restorer will want to grab the correct one. Rim circumference varied over the years, as the first two wheels to the right demonstrate. *James Mann*

emerged was for auction in 1997. Tuckett bought it, changed the oil, bands, and hoses. The car then started and drove, after more than 60 years idle. Rusty will never be restored, not in Tuckett's hands. He was an early advocate of not restoring functioning vehicles.

The garage housing Tuckett's operations is a modern agricultural building. The main area is 5,000 square feet, with lean-tos on either side. He keeps about 22 Model Ts on one side and 10 on the

In the 1980s, a Manchester man was restoring Model Ts. It took him a number of months, but he told a local reporter he could do it in six weeks if left alone. The reporter said, "If you can do that, I'll write a story about it." The restorer did, and this was the car he built. *James Mann*

The Golden Ford, minus its brass body, came with a load of parts Tuckett bought from an old Model T dealer in England. Only when he saw the registration plate in a book, affixed to a striking race car, did he realize he had something very special on hand. *James Mann*

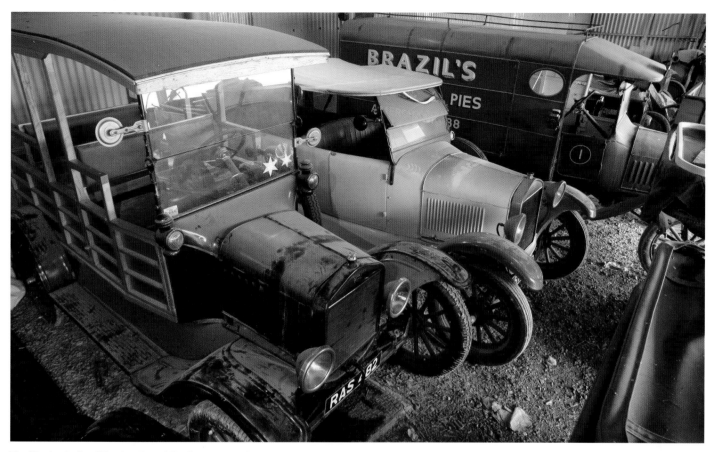

It all started with the Brazil's Sausages & Pies truck—the vehicle Tuckett repaired for his great-uncle, who bought it new in 1924. The wood-bodied depot hack in the foreground was built for Ford's centenary in 2003. It was constructed in the U.K. by residents at a village for mentally handicapped adults, who received a prize for their outstanding workmanship. *James Mann*

other. There are 30-plus antique Fords on the premises at any given time, plus lots of bits. New stock and good used parts are cataloged on the computer and shelved, while second-grade components are in piles wherever there is space. He and his crew draw from the piles as needed. Tuckett replenishes stores with trips around England and Europe, and also the United States. Vehicles and parts find him too, as his reputation spreads, some more than once.

Early cars aren't the only business in Tuckett's life. There's also the farm a quarter-mile up the road, where he lives with his wife, Mary. She runs the farm, while he handles the Fords. "Model Ts are a low-cost operation," he says, "but I'll never get rich from it. The workshop helps prop up the farming."

And what do the neighbors think of this business fixing up automobiles from the early part of the last century? "It tends to be a curiosity," Tuckett says. He's had no complaints. Wrenches turning and antique engines chuffing are quieter than a full-scale farming operation. It isn't the realization of a childhood dream, but being Europe's top Model T specialist suits Tuckett well—even if it never yields big money. "We have a lovely way of life," he says. "We're privileged to live on a nice spot in this world."

Delwyn Mallett

THE "TROUBLE" WITH MODERNISM

The Malletts live in half of a divided house, built by
well-known twentieth-century architect Harold Falkner
for a wealthy newspaperman who had returned to England
after editing a New Delhi paper. The upper portion of the
coach house–style garage offers dry storage for auto parts.
James Mann

The Bentley 1955 R-type Continental has served Mallett and his wife well. He calls it one of the great cars of all time, with excellent comfort and handling. Lurking behind is a rare Honda 125 Benly. Mallet has two of the little roadburners, each with interesting race bits. The plan is to build one bike with all the best parts. Someday. *James Mann*

In the 1970s, Mallett used the 300SL Mercedes as his daily driver. Beyond is a tool brand familiar in the United States. Mallett says, "Every mechanic worth his salt in Britain has Snap-on." *James Mann*

Delwyn Mallett has a problem—one we can all understand. These pretty cars with their curvy bodies and fancy names keep making trouble between him and the missus. Wouldn't be an issue if they'd keep their distance, but they come 'round his place, always with the understanding that he said they could stay. If the problem has led to a few nights in the doghouse, it's also produced an unusual collection of significant cars, with a few recurring themes.

In the 1960s Mallett went to art school, where he developed a taste for Modernism, especially the Bauhaus design ethic. Porsche's lines met his vision of an exciting car. A 356A coupe was his first of the marque, which he upgraded to from a secondhand Mini, his first car. "In the 1960s, Porsches were not at all fashionable and were rare in Britain," he explains. "Most people thought them overbodied, streamlined VWs." He sold that one after a year, hoping for a Speedster.

In 1969 he found a red one, which he bought and took on his honeymoon. "I still have the car and the wife, though she may leave me because I have too many cars," he jokes. This Speedster is a rare right-hand-drive model. The underside had seen some rot, though, which he realized was extensive when the driver's seat fell through the bottom of the car while he was driving it. He bought another one, planning to cannibalize it to restore his first. But it was too good. So now that car, which is silver, is also a permanent boarder.

Still after a driver, Mallett bought a pale blue Porsche—which he still owns, of course. It wasn't running, but he figured he could get it on the road in three months. The renovation stretched to 28 years, which casts a little light on his wife's concerns.

We all know how projects get bumped down the to-do list. Other cars coming aboard are a primary culprit. How could Mallett, a German sports car enthusiast, not pick up a Mercedes Gullwing when that Siren struck up a tune? The Gullwing entered his life in 1972 and became his everyday car.

His interest in Porsches didn't decline, but it did evolve. He learned of the Porsche family's friendship with Carlo Abarth and became fixated on an Abarth Porsche. These were the lightened, streamlined 356B Carrera GTs that set fire to Le Mans and the Targa Florio in the early 1960s. After missing one for £800 in the early 1970s, Mallett picked up a half-dozen Fiat Abarths of various types and tune.

More Porsche digging led Mallett to Hans Ledwinka, a contemporary of Ferdinand Porsche's applying the same design principles. Both men were renowned engineers of their day, Porsche at his company in Germany, and Ledwinka at Tatra in Czechoslovakia. Ledwinka's legacy was another air-cooled, rear-engined car with a striking Modernist design. Needless to say, Mallett had to have one. As luck would have it—what sort of luck, his wife might dispute—he was doing some advertising work in Prague. He bought a model T603 there, then bought a T87 from a friend who had picked it up and had it restored in the Czech Republic.

The Mallett collection is not just marked by similarities, but also stark differences. Take his Cord, which he describes as "a good bookend with the Tatra." Where the latter is an oversteering, light-nosed, air-cooled, rear-engine, rear-drive machine, the Cord is understeering, nose-heavy, water-cooled, front-engine, front-drive. "It gives me an inner glow of satisfaction to know that they're diametrically opposed in every dimension," Mallett quips. Besides, when he went to look at it, he concluded, "It's such a beautiful piece of 1930s design, I've got to have it around."

Perhaps the car that's brought him the most trouble is his Studebaker. He's always loved American coupes of the 1930s, especially the 1936–1937 "Bat-Window" Stude. He had been looking for one for several years, when he found one for sale at a rally in the 1980s. A "young lad" had imported it from South Africa. Mallett arranged to meet him in downtown London by his advertising offices off Piccadilly Circus. He negotiated the deal through his office number, because his wife had threatened the D-word "if he couldn't get his car habit under control."

Mallett met him at an underground garage with several thousand British pounds in cash in his pocket. But the car wouldn't start, so they had to push it out into London traffic and pop-start it. The young man wanted to get a last picture of it with his girlfriend, who loved the car and worked nearby. Concerned about the traffic, and the fact that this car was not licensed or taxed for use on English roads, Mallett consented only anxiously.

When the seller reappeared not with his girlfriend but sandwiched between a couple of icy-faced bobbies, Mallett's

There are 1 1/2 Abarths in this photo. In front of the Fiat, what looks like a section of ladder from a fire truck is actually a tubular space frame for an Abarth 1000SP sports racer. *James Mann*

Mallett's space includes the main garage plus an open carpark to one side. Space is tight, so he moves cars regularly as projects tussle at the top of the to-do list. Motorcycles, like his BMW R69S, jostle for their bit of real estate as well.
James Mann

He loves the styling of the Cord, but says, "It doesn't want to go around any curve you point it at." The covered car beside it is a special-bodied racing Abarth Bialbero. *James Mann*

mind started reeling—was the young man a crook? A drug dealer? Was the unlicensed vehicle Mallett was standing beside filled with contraband? When he inquired in his most respectful voice what the problem was, one of the "coppers" told him to fly off, with slightly different wording. Mallett paused, then chased after them and inquired again. This time he got the same response, louder, plus a shove in the chest and a threat that he too would be arrested if he didn't disappear.

After a longer cooling off period, Mallett went to inquire at the station, only to learn the seller, dashing through the financial district to get his girlfriend for the last Stude photo, had been wrongly grabbed over a purse snatching. He had been

released, and Mallett couldn't find him. Tired from the day's adventure, Mallett decided to get the Studebaker off the street, so he swapped it into his paid parking space downtown.

Next day, he found the seller, closed the deal, and seemed to have the game won. He had the car, he had the title. His wife had no idea.

Since the car was taking up his one paid parking spot, Mallett covered by riding his Moto Guzzi to work—rain or shine. But his wife didn't like him riding the bike (and that's when she didn't know why he was doing it). After a few months, judgment day came. The garage owner thought the old Yank was starting to look like an abandoned car and told Mallett to clear it out.

Graceful curves mark almost every vehicle in the Mallett collection, which includes several motorcycles, like the Moto Guzzi Mk1 Le Mans at right, as well as the "shoebox" 1950 Ford Custom coupe by the hedge outside. *James Mann*

He hoped inspiration, in the form of a very fine explanation for this new purchase, would strike him on the way home. It didn't. What struck instead were the karmic forces that punish men sneaking about against their wife's will. The 40-mile journey home was basically flat and straight but for a single steep and twisting unlit hill alongside a ridge with no shoulder. At 11 p.m. the South African Stude died in the middle of this hill.

Mallett hopped out in a blind curve and ran backward as cars screeched to a halt for this dimly visible, arm-waving advertising man in a black suit. He took off his jacket and shivered in his white shirt, slightly more visible, until an unamused traffic

patrol officer appeared on the scene. Mallett explained his immediate concerns and with the officer's help, backed the car down the hill to a pull-off spot, at which point the officer lost interest and drove away.

Advertising people were among the first in the workforce to adopt cell phones, though in the 1980s, they were brick-sized. Mallett hoisted his and placed a call home. "Darling, I know this means divorce, but I've bought another car and I've broken down on the Hog's Back and need. . . ." The rest of the sentence was truncated when she hung up the phone—and left it off the hook. Mallett crawled into his just desserts and rested for an hour or two. Then he decided to see if circumstances

Porsche's creation faces Ledwinka's. The Porsche's spats, which Mallett had custom made, are replicas of those worn by the early aluminum-bodied, Austrian-built Gmund Porsches that raced at Le Mans. He has a Judson supercharger for the car too, which he plans to fit as a period curiosity. *James Mann*

Red Speedster was Mallett's second Porsche, in which he took his honeymoon. He also campaigned the car in some vintage racing events earlier in its life. *James Mann*

The Studebaker's tiny taillights were too small to offer comfort when the car broke down in the middle of a winding hill on its maiden voyage home. The cutaway 3.0 CSL poster came from a friend who worked for a BMW dealer. Mallet loves the "Batmobile" but has never owned one. The bike below it with the wraparound front fender is a 50-cc Itom, which Mallett bought specifically for that design touch. *James Mann*

The former ad man also paints. He has produced a limited edition set of prints of the Gmund Porsches that raced at Le Mans in 1951, 1952, and 1953. He also paints the Mercedes and Auto Union Silver Arrows of the 1930s. The picture behind him is of the Auto Union Avus "streamliner." *James Mann*

might finally be done kicking his backside. The Stude started, he drove it home, and but for three months' stone silence from his wife, all has been well since.

The Malletts live in a home designed by well-known British architect, Harold Falkner. Between the garage and the adjoining carport he nearly has room for about 9 1/2 cars (the half being a disassembled Abarth tube-frame race car). They're all old cars. Mallett has never owned a new one. He doesn't dislike them—his list of models he'd like to own includes an Audi TT and Porsche Cayman—but every time he's had the money for a car, he's always bought something old.

Those days are changing, though, and Mallett's been thinking about getting rid of some of the old stuff—like the Abarths. If he does decide to go that route, someone else will have a shot at some cool projects, and Mallett will have some more space for his other cars. His might not be the only sigh of relief when they go.

Along with cars, Mallett enjoys photography and old cameras. The camera is a 1932 Zeiss Contax—"If Leica was the Mercedes-Benz of 35-millimeter cameras, this was the Auto Union. The two cameras slugged it out for supremacy during the 1930s—just as the cars did." The picture is his daughter with her Beetle cabriolet, which she no longer uses but for some strange reason refuses to leave. *James Mann*

Dick Shepard

BASTOGNE AND BEYOND

This 1954 REO troop carrier came from the U.S. Army in Germany. The chain could be used for pulling and towing, while the black bar provided a rigid coupling for towing or pushing. Flags on the workshop wall include the 101st and 82nd Airborne Divisions, two famous American units that fought in the Battle of the Bulge. *James Mann*

The trucks in the field were motorized work horses, carrying everything the soldiers did not have on their backs or in their hands. Mounted on the fender, this first aid kit was both readily accessible and visible when needed. *James Mann*

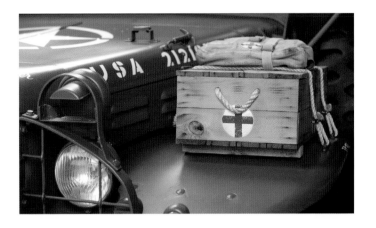

Dick Shepard was not in World War II, at least not as a soldier. But his family's farm lay next to an American Air Force base in England. If you had a large house during that period, you were often asked to board people involved in the war effort. The Shepards provided lodging for two such people—a young

The Dodge weapons carrier is a sturdy rig. Shepard often wears khaki clothing, but at 6 feet and 16 stone (224 pounds) he has yet to find a military uniform that fits him comfortably. *James Mann*

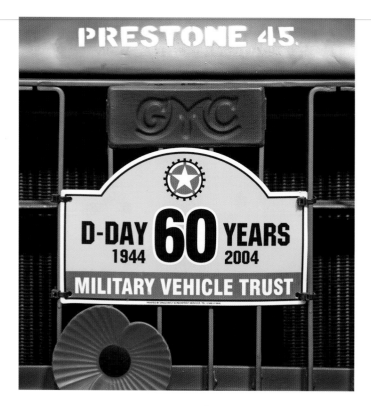

woman war correspondent, and the captain of an American B-17 bomber crew.

Shepard was only six years old when the visitors took up residence with them, but the woman who stayed there made an impression on him. Her family back in the States had a larger impact as publishers of the *New York Times*. The young woman was Ruth Sulzberger, daughter of Arthur Hays Sulzberger. She stayed with the Shepard family from 1943 to 1945, and she married that B-17 captain and returned to a life of journalism in the United States after the war.

You couldn't live through World War II and not be influenced by it. Shepard took a liking to the vehicles, particularly American-made trucks. "I like my GMCs," he says. His first purchase was a Willys Jeep in 1972. He has collected military vehicles ever since, though he bought and sold earlier in his life. The trucks he has retained date from World War II and the Cold War. All get used. He takes them to local rallies and shows, and he ventures to Europe a couple of times a year to partake in important celebrations related to the war. The ones that will travel at a decent road speed, he drives; otherwise, they go on a "low loader," or a flatbed as we would call it in the United States.

Even though the war is more than a half-century gone, Shepard describes the interest in military vehicles as "very, very strong in England and Europe." Some enthusiasts are military

What Americans might call a tanker truck, British forces called a "petrol bowser." This 1943 GMC petrol bowser was used in the film *Memphis Belle*. *James Mann*

Shepard's pontoon boat has been in the local papers, seen here as it was shown in a display of thousands of war vehicles in Kent. These trucks still equipped with their pontoons are rare. Shepard's rig is one of about 25 truck and pontoon sets known to remain. *James Mann*

veterans, while others who survived the war as civilians, and their children, carry on maintaining and showing these machines for the memories and principles they represent. The crowd is too big for Shepard to know everyone, but he has many close friends who share his passion for finding, restoring, and preserving these pieces of history.

Preservation is an important role for collectors who focus on military vehicles. "You can't leave them out," Shepard emphasizes; "They deteriorate if you do." He houses his collection in a 6,000-square-foot warehouse built for that purpose. Even sheltered, the vehicles need ongoing attention. "There's always something to do," he says. "A little rust that needs repairing . . . I can never really say I'm completely done with one."

Much of the work he does himself, but he's backed off somewhat from his adventuresome rebuilding days of old. War vehicles are tricky because on one hand, they're classic technology, which is simple in its elements—plugs, points, carburetors, clutches, manual transmissions. But military hardware is also specialized to meet demands beyond those imposed on regular street vehicles. "In the past I've messed about with things I didn't understand," Shepard laughs, "and it's cost me a lot of money. When I got the parts back together, I always had nuts and bolts left over." He hasn't diminished his efforts—he just brought in a mechanic to be sure everything goes back together the way it was before it came apart.

This 1944 GMC truck carries a Leroi petrol-engine compressor. These trucks were used by engineers in the war. Shepard added the ring mount and .50-caliber Browning machine gun, purchased from a man in Belgium. Though real, the gun is deactivated. *James Mann*

Owner Shepard did most of the work on his 1940 GMC short-wheelbase hard cab, which he took on the Liberation Run rally in July 2006. One hundred vehicles made the run, visiting sites of the Normandy invasion and finishing in Bastogne, site of the Battle of the Bulge, which broke Hitler's final offensive of the war. *James Mann*

A good example of what happens from neglect, and can be undone with care and elbow grease, is his 1944 GMC compressor truck. A French collector had it stowed in a barn 20 miles north of Paris, where it had sat for many decades. When the French collector passed away, Shepard bought the vehicle from the man's widow. The engine had seized and the rest of the running and stopping gear needed attention, along with many other areas of the truck. Shepard brought it back on a low-loader—his home is only 70 miles from France—and then embarked on an eight-month restoration. Today everything works as it did when engineers used the truck during the war. Shepard is comfortable running it at 35 to 40 miles per hour, and he drives the truck to area rallies.

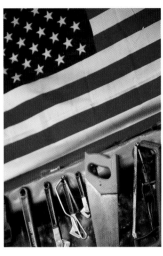

All of the U.S. military trucks in the Shepard collection were built by a nation of 48 states, before Alaska and Hawaii joined the union. This flag has the World War II star count. The workshop is well equipped to handle virtually any repair. *James Mann*

Longer distances don't put him off, nor does poor weather. In the spirit of what soldiers went through to win the last world war, Shepard and others will trek in winter cold and snows to honor important battles. Every January he journeys to a rally in Bastogne, in the Ardennes forest, for commemoration of the Battle of the Bulge. There the Allies broke one of Hitler's final offensive campaigns of the war in December 1944 and January 1945. It is regarded as one of the most important confrontations of the war, and is described on a monument in Arlington National Cemetery in Washington, D.C., as "the greatest land battle in the history of the United States Army." American casualties were about

A 5-ton 1956 American REO wrecker, used by the U.S. Army in Germany during the Cold War. The air cleaner exiting the top side of the engine bay gives a good sense of how deep this truck could be immersed in water and remain running. *James Mann*

During the Cold War, this 1953 Bedford "Green Goddess" utility truck was available to address any sabotage of communication systems. At the time the trucks were sold in the 1960s and 1970s, they were still the property of the U.S. government, Shepard says. *James Mann*

This 1944 GMC Pontoon Carrier was used by the 552nd Engineering Corps to build bridges across the Rhine River. The 552nd Engineering Corps was attached to the 7th Army, which General George S. Patton had commanded before leading the 3rd Army in 1944. Behind the GMC are about 10 British telephone boxes that Shepard picked up several years ago as the government began replacing them. *James Mann*

81,000, British 1,400, and German as many as 100,000. Shepard says the annual remembrance rally is usually very cold with lots of snow—fitting, as the Battle of the Bulge was fought in the coldest temperatures that had ever been recorded in the region.

There was a time when Shepard sold, as well as bought, military vehicles. "When I was younger, if it showed a profit, it had to go," he admits. "Now I'm not worried about profit." The World War II collection includes the 1944 compressor truck, a 1940 GMC short-wheelbase hard cab, a 1942 Dodge weapons carrier, a 1943 GMC "petrol bowser" (fuel truck), and a 1944 GMC pontoon truck. From the Cold War are two 1953 Bedford "Green Goddess" auxiliary trucks, a 1954 REO troop carrier with multifuel diesel engine, and 1956 American REO wrecker. He has some other curiosities, too, like 10 British telephone boxes, down from an initial 50.

Shepard has a few vehicles that he's still searching for, too. One on his list is an M20 Greyhound, the light armored reconnaissance vehicle made by Ford. They look a bit like tanks with wheels and tires instead of tracks for higher speeds. These were nimble creations capable of 60 miles per hour, Shepard says, and outfitted with ring mounts and machine guns to help escape any run-ins with the enemy. Shepard looked at one in Belgium, but the seller wanted too much for it. "I shall find one," he says. He is always on the lookout for special vehicles.

The collection is likely to grow, and to continue for many years, as Shepard's three sons have also taken an interest in military trucks. "Two of them have one jeep each, and one has a weapons carrier," he says. The war that affected millions of lives in Europe and beyond will not be forgotten, nor, thanks to collectors like Shepard, will the vehicles that rumbled through the mud and snow and made victory possible.

MAKE IT FAST, MAKE IT YOUR OWN

Those who never seek excellence are content to do without it. Join the quest, however, and you will pursue it to your final day.

Ron Jolliffe

ROCKET SCIENCE

This '49 Olds gave Jolliffe's shop its name. This car has run at Bonneville and on Southern California's dry lakes to a top speed of a bit over 170 miles per hour. While this is a working garage, some decoration is welcome here, such as the '57 Bel Air profile and Mobile Company's commercial art. Jolliffe was an art teacher before turning to the wrench and micrometer full time. *Peter Vincent*

People have asked him if he's a nuclear physicist, but not the ones who have been to the garage. This is no particle accelerator—just a well-equipped shop to fix 'em, paint 'em, and turn 'em loose on the roads or the Bonneville Salt Flats. *Peter Vincent*

"The car gets shorter."

This is not Ron Jolliffe's secret for squeaking that last collectible into a crowded garage. It's his description of what happens when you push a 70-year-old hot rod from 220 to 240 miles per hour at the Bonneville Salt Flats. "It darts around," he adds, "it just takes a little bit of wind gust. Speed exaggerates these motions."

Jolliffe spends a lot of time pondering speed, and it's paid off. He's earned two separate speed records for cars and one for motorcycles on his beloved salt flats. The latter is less than half the rate of his hot rod dashes, but he calls whipping his old Vincent Shadow to record speed "the scariest ride of my life, at 105 miles per hour."

His garage is tied to such thoughts, a place where wrenches and principles of aerodynamics and horsepower turn. Apart from the roughly 10 cumulative minutes of runtime he gets at Bonneville each year, plus a lot more time in transportation,

This shot pretty well sums up the garage, as well as its owner's passions—building cool hot rods and powerful engines, and riding and tweaking great bikes. *Peter Vincent*

Jolliffe quit teaching after a quarter-century and moved to Idaho to open a shop rebuilding and hopping up cars and motorcycles. He calls it Rocket Science Engineering, or, as here, the Rocket Speed Shop. *Peter Vincent*

Jolliffe builds cars, engines, and bikes for customers. He's spent the last 10 to 15 years building street rods and restoring antique motorcycles, mostly British. Lately he's been shifting his focus more toward race engines.

Cars are a first love, but a second career for Jolliffe. He taught art in his prior life, primarily ceramics and some print making. He enjoyed that job—did it for 25 years—but cars started to dominate his thoughts. He took on some restoration work, mostly foreign, mostly Porsches. It would take him about a year to do one car. Then he'd take on another. Customers were happy, and so was he. Finally, he quit teaching and moved to Idaho to do cars full time.

"My dad loved to work on cars," remembers Jolliffe. They worked on cars a lot together, whenever time permitted. Jolliffe's father was an Air Force pilot, and he'd go overseas for a while, then return and get right back under the hood. During high school, Jolliffe went through between 10 and 20 cars. He didn't see it as a professional calling at that time, but old habits die hard and first loves are slow to fade.

People around Hailey, Idaho—and hot rodders and speed freaks at points much further—know Jolliffe's place as the Rocket Science garage. He didn't coin the name. It comes from a magazine article about a 1949 Oldsmobile Rocket 88 he built to run at Bonneville. The editor penned the title and Jolliffe liked it, not just for the piece but as a larger statement of his passion for cars, especially

Another passion for this teacher-turned-tuner is motorcycles, in particular the Vincent. This original, unrestored 1954 Black Shadow holds the Bonneville record for completely stock, vintage motorcycles with 1,000-cc displacement. Jolliffe pushed it to 105 miles per hour for the timed mile, but he says "a smaller rider, with more courage, could easily boost that to something over 120." *Peter Vincent*

Looking for Ron Jolliffe? Try the garage. He's owned this 1954 Mercedes-Benz cabriolet with prewar coachwork for many years. It sports a postwar six-cylinder engine like the ones in the famous 300SL Gullwing. He's been working on this restoration for 15 years, with lots of interruptions to build race cars and engines for himself and others. *Peter Vincent*

Oldsmobiles, and moving fast. Sometimes it gets taken too literally—he's had people in town ask, "Are you really a nuclear physicist?"

As a working garage, the Rocket Science shop is especially representative of its owner. His career and his hobby overlap and blend together indistinguishably. For the most part it's an orderly operation, but Jolliffe isn't a neat freak. "I'll get excited about some facet of something I'm doing and reach for the next tool. By 2 a.m. I've got something I'm grinning at and a big mess. I don't think you can get a lot built if you're always worrying about neatness."

Scattered tools is a separate issue from dirty jobs. Jolliffe's shop handles both pretty well. He has two spaces—one is home to mechanical tasks, while the other houses body work, paint and fabrication. It's still a struggle. As Jolliffe puts it, "You're always fighting one job's dirt with the next job's need for cleanliness." Bonneville's a special challenge because the cars return covered with a fine layer of salt. The only way to address it is to get them on a lift for a thorough steam cleaning. You don't let rust get to a vehicle you're looking to drive at a rate of a mile in 15 seconds.

Not all of Jolliffe's vehicles are Bonneville cars. In addition to the record-setting '34 Ford roadster race car, he has a '32 Ford roadster and a '40 coupe—three cars he always wanted to own. Sometimes he takes them all in and appreciates the fact that he never dreamed, when they first caught his eye, that he would one day have not just one but the full trio. In addition, he has a couple of old Mercedes-Benz cabriolets. The Benzes have appreciated nicely in recent years, and he will likely sell one to pay for a new shop he's planning in California's central coast. He's paid his dues in the Idaho snows and is ready for a climate that allows him to work and drive outside all year round.

In building hot rods, Jolliffe will do what the customer wants, but he has his own preferences. Esthetically, he likes things that draw their form from old race cars. He prefers his coupes unchopped and wants the general profile and silhouette to stay close to the original. On the floor he believes "real hot rods have three pedals." When he was a kid listening to guys

Chances are you like your work if your rec room is attached to your place of business. Does Jolliffe take a break from work to catch a show or read a mag, or does he take a break from TV or an article to turn a few wrenches? Both. *Peter Vincent*

Is it 12:30 p.m. or a.m.? Jolliffe admits that when exciting things start coming apart or going back together, the clock hands can turn deep into the night and he won't even notice. The bike is a 1968 BSA Victor 441-cc single that used to be a racer but is now a "too pretty" trail bike. *Peter Vincent*

Jolliffe's desk is no stranger to Bonneville photos, or photos, books and memorabilia related to hot rod culture. He collects old cameras, too, like the Rolleiflex Twin Lens Reflex shown. *Peter Vincent*

pull out of the drive-in in their hot rods, that's what they had—shifting is part of the hot rod tradition, with its own distinctive tune as you go through the gears.

Fancy paint jobs aren't his style. He can appreciate the work, but it's wasted effort in light of another of his views—that "a hot rod needs to be sideways on a gravel road to fulfill its destiny."

He's fond of '49–'56 Oldsmobiles and has a huge collection of those engines and speed equipment for them. Crate engines don't do much for him: "There's something more satisfying in pushing the starter button on a 60-year-old engine that runs like a dream." Hunting down old parts is another enjoyable part of his job. "It's a great thrill when you find old rocker arms that sat in a speed shop for 50 years."

In addition to V-8s, Jolliffe also likes 1950s GMC straight sixes. He's putting two together for a new assault on Bonneville. He'll put them in his '34 race car successively, one with forced induction, one without.

A few vintage performance manifolds join hot rod art, including dual-quad, twin-two barrel and six-two-barrel! Is that a "twelve pack"?! There's a phrase that's sure to get a scowl from law enforcement. *Peter Vincent*

Modifying the intake manifold for better airflow is an old-time speed trick, practiced here, along with many others. Jolliffe is particularly fond of Oldsmobile engines, of which he has a large store, plus vintage speed parts for them. This old Edelbrock four-carb manifold fits an early Olds V-8. *Peter Vincent*

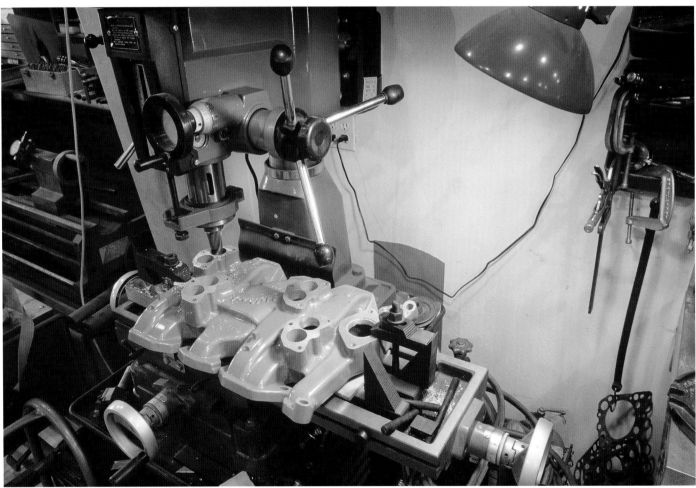

Jolliffe likes fast hot rods, running a few for himself and building them for customers. This is the Rocket Science 1934 Ford Roadster Bonneville car, built on a custom tube frame fitted with a 1060 HP Merlin Pro Stock–style engine. It holds two Bonneville class records and has never made a run under 200 miles per hour, except to license a new driver for speed runs. *Peter Vincent*

The "six" with a high-tech centrifugal supercharger on it will make over 600 horsepower. Jolliffe hopes that powerplant can push the six-cylinder record over the 200-mile per hour mark. He thinks the normally aspirated lump can move the car into the 180-mile per hour range.

Some people might not understand a fixation with building a car to move just a little faster than a prior one like it, in the middle of Utah on a flat expanse of salt. But the jobs that those people have wouldn't likely hold much interest for a gearhead speed freak, either. As he tinkers in a shop amid a pile of tools in the wee hours of the morning, looking for a tweak that sits just right, Jolliffe is at peace. "I'm sure I'm doing what I should be doing," he says. And while some folks yearn for that first day of summer each year, Jolliffe looks forward to a later date, when an event called Speed Week goes down in Utah—"I'm counting the days till August."

Mark Morton

A HOT RODDER'S HOT RODDER

There's a reason Southern California real estate is a hot commodity, and this is it: a beautiful house and a beautiful garage that can be enjoyed year round with the doors up and the cars out. *Robert Genat*

The car motif features outside as well with this Steve Posson sculpture of Frank Lockhart's Miller 91 Indy Racer from the 1920s. Several other Posson works decorate the library. *Robert Genat*

Scientists have not identified it yet, but there is a garage factor that attaches to the blood and shapes the lives of those who bear it. They will be car people, wrench turners, men who measure roads and spaces for their ability to draw out or set off a fine automobile—where "fine" is a matter of taste. Mark Morton is garage positive. As his signoff at the end of a piece in his online magazine, *Hop Up*, puts it: "It's about the iron . . . always has been."

Today, Morton has plenty of iron. Beautiful iron. Hot rod and custom iron built up the way he likes it—with vintage parts. It's come from hard work and good fortune, and he's thankful for every vehicle the two have brought him.

His father ran a garage in Bell Gardens, California, but it wasn't nurture that gave him his love of cars; he was born with it. Morton was obsessed with them before he knew the words to express it. "I was the kid with the rubber car in his pocket," he says. You know the kid—the one sitting in the pedal car in the old photos, with a couple more toy cars in his hands.

He was born too late to storm the dry lakes with the hot rod pioneers, but it was their handiwork and lifestyle that captured Morton's imagination. They did a lot with a little, putting time, sweat, and innovation into their cars and getting a lot of speed and style in return. Hot rodders were cool—maybe the first crowd to give that word its slang meaning.

Plenty of fluorescent and track lighting, plus light-colored walls and floor, make the Morton collection easy to see and appreciate, like this '29 Roadster and mild custom '65 Riviera. *Robert Genat*

Rods aplenty include green Joe Mac Model A Sport Coupe, T tub homage to Tom Hynes and the Archies, dark blue '23 T roadster, plus black coupe, which Morton has been driving around the country in stages (leaving it with friends along the way), and roadster Rodzy, also regularly driven. *Robert Genat*

Morton's first set of wheels was a '38 Ford pickup with a souped-up flathead. He traded that for a 210 Del Rey coupe with a 265 V-8 that his father built. These were good cars and good projects. Yet it would be a few years before he could start to accumulate the sorts of cars that fired his imagination even more.

Some guys find the means to collect through cars themselves, be they dealers, customizers, or aftermarket suppliers. Other enthusiasts strike off for opportunities outside their passion, yet fuel their drive for success with visions of cars they long to own. It's been about 20 years since Morton's mobile offices company became successful enough that he could start collecting cars. And he's done it with zeal ever since.

Hot rods and customs are an important part of the collection, naturally, but his interests reach out to other classic and antique cars. He's deliberate, rather than impulsive, as a buyer, with lists of autos of the types that interest him. Each new increment of success with his business represents a chance to seek out a car on the list. As Morton puts it, "My passion and my scheme to collect anticipate my ability to pay for them."

This garage not only features a cool Stetson sign, but the Lincoln owned by G. Henry Stetson himself. The original pink slip is part of the wall art, too, though not in this shot. *Robert Genat*

The road map holder is a nice accessory from an earlier time's commercial garage—a Mobil gas station. Period maps make the holder more interesting. Imagine how different that Los Angeles and vicinity map looks from today. *Robert*

Some garages expand with the collection; others are built to purpose. Morton's is the latter type. When it was time for a new house, his wife, Evonne—Morton's "partner in the accomplishment and enjoyment of it all"—found many that were suitable for their personal needs; but none was sufficient to house the cars. So Morton built a home to accommodate all that he had, a dozen and a half beautiful machines.

There's one more spot on the property that he's eyeing for a "garage annex." This will need to be excavated and should yield space for another four big cars—or perhaps as many as eight small ones, plus a walk-in wine cellar, with a sod roof garden on top. That project is a few more business deals away— and good inspiration for making them. His next wish-list purchase is to be a brass-era car, ideally a Stutz Bearcat or Mercer

This 1930s sprint car features a Clyde Adams frame, period cowling, DO (dual-overhead) Hal cylinder head conversion on a Model B four-cylinder Ford engine, and Dayton drop-center wire wheels. *Robert Genat*

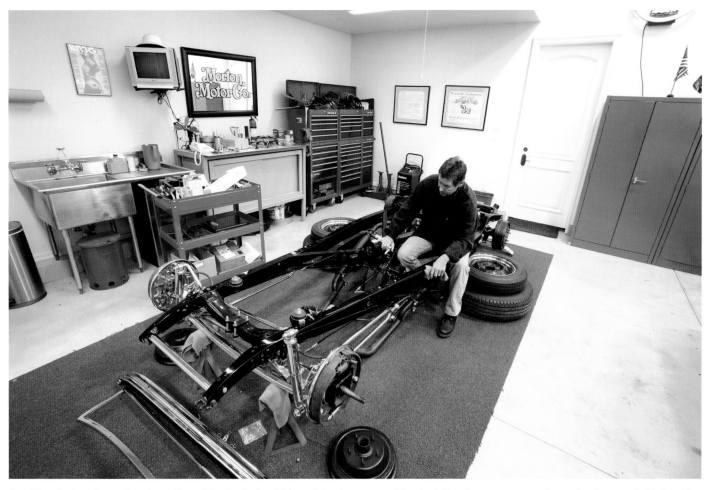

Another hot rod coming together. Morton's traditional tastes are evident at the four corners—drum brakes, not disks. He likes to build them the way the old guard did when hot rods first hit the scene. *Robert Genat*

Raceabout. More likely it will be something more easily attained, like a 1915 Cadillac or perhaps a Buick roadster.

Morton's present space is austere, with little artwork on the walls and none of the bric-a-brac that accumulates in a typical enthusiast's garage—which is not to say he has none. "I have as much art and ephemera as anyone," he laughs. But it's stored elsewhere where it doesn't compete with the cars, and vice versa. The few pieces that do adorn the walls are genuine articles, like the vehicles themselves. They include the poster for the last race at Ascot Speedway, and a work that Peter Vincent did. He also displays the pink slips from some of his cars. The slip from his 1933 Lincoln KB Judkins Coupe is a fun one. It was originally owned by "lid" magnate G. Henry Stetson, whose listed street address is Rancho Sombrero.

It's not a museum atmosphere—these cars are driven—but it's tidy. Among the 16 slots is a 2-1/2-story section where the cars can be "stacked," and also examined and worked on comfortably on lifts. Still, the home garage is reserved for "clean" work. The greasy, oily, teardown-type of stuff is done off-site at a spot Morton calls "the barn."

Do you go with a clock in your garage, or is your time there your own? If you need to keep track of the hour, a vintage clock is a good way to do it. This one complements the Mobil maps. *Robert Genat*

The garage is a retreat as well as storage space, a place where Morton is drawn to enjoy his vehicles. Sometimes that means a drive, but as often he finds pleasure in these cars without the vroom and rumble. The garage has a very good sound system of its own and is well lit to showcase this dream assemblage. A perfectly good end to a hardworking day for Morton is just through the door from the house: "I put on some music, get a cigar and a glass of whiskey, and go out into the garage, thanking my lucky stars."

There's another Mark Morton too, along with the businessman and the collector relaxing among his mechanical treasures. That's Morton the high priest—or at least agent provocateur—of the "Tabernacle of Gow." Gow is a blood protein, a strain of the garage factor. It's also a term from Morton's revered hot-rod era, when sayings like "Fords for Gow, Chevies for Plow" were well-known taunts. Perhaps at first it was a youthful speed-freak's inflection of "go," as in that car's got a lotta gow. Today it stands for "gospel of wheels" and the Tabernacle of Gow is Morton's online publication, *Hop Up*, dedicated to the spirit of hot rodding during its earliest days.

Here the cars and the tricks and the ideals that made that era great live on in cyberspace, as photos and stories of

Hop Up was one of the earliest hot rod publications, filled with customization and speed tips, parts, and tricks. Morton revived it on the web and as an annual magazine featuring traditional hot rods and customs. The *Hop Up* panel wagon is parked in the two-story portion of the garage, where vehicles can be raised for underside work. *Robert Genat*

If you're into cars, you're into car books. Morton has an excellent collection, and the surroundings for thumbing through them aren't so bad either. It's easier to make time for those new acquisitions you've been planning to read in a library like this. *Robert Genat*

hot rod excitement old and new. It's a focal point, a figurative watering hole, for fans of hot rods in the old-school style, built up with flathead motors, drum brakes, and iron and steel instead of billet. Morton's got plenty of friends from across the ideological tracks, but his passion is the way the cars were hopped up first. This is the love that made the man that built

the garage that houses the cars that somehow also make the man.

His collection is a fulfilled dream, he says, but it's also an organism and it has to grow. "I revel in my good fortune. I know people way up the ladder from me, but there are a lot of guys not as lucky." A man who knows what he has can enjoy it the most, and Morton's garage is a perfect place to do so.

Chuck de Heras

RODS & WURLITZERS

One of the benefits of California's warm, dry, bug-free days is that you can leave your doors up and have the horizon as your garage wall, which de Heras often does. Throw in some classic jukebox music, and it's easy to see why this is Chuck de Heras' favorite spot. *Robert Genat*

If it's old and mechanical, chances are Chuck de Heras is interested in it. He may not buy, if you're selling, but he'd probably like to know how it works. When he does bring something home, whether it's a hot rod or an old jukebox, he'll take it apart and find out. "I like to tinker," de Heras says, and though his hot rods have filled magazine pages both here and abroad, he enjoys working on the cars more than driving them.

This is not to say de Heras doesn't like to put his foot in it. He does—and he's got some cars that can get up and move. But as he observes with a little remorse, "The places where you can do that are starting to disappear." Maybe that's why de Heras wants his cars drivable and streetable, even the fast ones. He's always got a few cars going together, a few more in the planning and parts-gathering stage, and an eye for other machinery that incorporates some cleverness or ingenuity he admires.

Before he had cars, De Heras started collecting coin-operated music machines. He owns the jukebox from *Happy Days*. How cool is that? And he didn't buy it from the set; the studio rented it from him—de Heras knew it was cool first. We call them jukeboxes, but some of his machines predate that term, going back to the second decade of the twentieth century, when records first came out. These earliest players lack speakers, using gramophone-style trumpets instead.

Who coined the term "jukebox," and when, is as insoluble as the same debate about the origin of "hot rod," but de Heras knows the background. It emerged from the south, where

A well-lit, well-equipped garage can host many intriguing projects, from hot rods to woodies, and jukeboxes to fancy antique scales. And when your eyes grow tired from staring at tiny parts, a row of windows offers a view of the rolling California landscape. *Robert Genat*

Framing the elegant Cadillac "Doctor's coupe" are a modified Whizzer motorized bicycle, good for a scary 35 to 40 miles per hour, and a 1932 Ford four-door high-boy sedan, chopped three inches. *Robert Genat*

people gathered in "juke joints" to dance, relax, and listen to music. Sometimes a juke joint was no more than a shack, which made a jukebox's compact size a lot more convenient than finding room for four or five musicians.

De Heras started his jukebox collection some 30 years ago. "I saw something at a swap meet," he recalls, "and that triggered it." Back then there were warehouses full of them, and you could go around the country and search out all kinds of great machines. He focused on Wurlitzers and has amassed a wonderful assortment. There is no complete collection of Wurlitzer models that anyone knows about, but de Heras is very close, lacking only two—one is so rare collectors debate whether it was ever built; the other, from 1938, had a production run of only 90 units. Today de Heras has about 100 coin-operated music players, of which 30 to 40 are restored.

He does most of the refinishing himself—the cabinet, the mechanical aspects—leaving only the amplifiers to someone with a strong electronics background. He has records for them too, lots of them, though he doesn't style himself a record collector. The very early stuff uses 78-rpm records, while the *Happy Days*–style machines play 45s. The music that's available tends to reflect the period when those machines were made, giving de Heras a lot of variety across his collection. Some of it's good, some he calls hokey. One of his machines features most of the big car songs, like Beach Boys stuff and "Hot Rod Lincoln." "That one gets used a lot," de Heras says. But he's not a fanatic about format or genre. If what he wants to hear is on a CD, that's what he plays. Sometimes the best thing to work to is silence.

The noncar collections came about in part because he didn't have the space for automobiles. But his interest in jukeboxes

This period Riley overhead-valve cylinder head and Scott supercharger go on an old four-banger Ford. The conversion was originally made for trucks to give them more power in the mountains, but was soon adopted by hot rodders to hop up cars too. *Robert Genat*

goes beyond convenient dimensions. "They pioneered a lot of things—colored plastic, polarized plastic that changed colors. All the functions the old machines perform were done mechanically," he notes. De Heras loves to see how they did things back then—to take these beautiful pieces apart, see how they work, and then restore them to prime condition.

When his kids were grown, de Heras shifted gears and moved to the country. There he built a working garage where he could house the cars he now had the room to collect, repair, modify, and restore. His 4,600-square-foot garage features generous doors to let in the Southern California light and air. Here, hot rods, soda machines, jukeboxes, and other tinkerabilia mingle with milling machines, grinders, hoists, and a glass-bead cabinet. There's another 4,500-square-foot space down below, on the back side of the property, to house additional vehicles and gadgetry.

One of his first projects for the new space was an extended Model A truck. He and some hot rod savants took a traditional

De Heras likes nothing more than to take some time out in the garage to be among his collection and to tinker with one of the cars or jukeboxes. *Robert Genat*

Drive-in movie theaters are as rare today as classic jukeboxes, another piece of a golden era for the automobile. Pacific Drive-in Theaters were a major chain on the West Coast during the outdoor-movie era. *Robert Genat*

Chuck de Heras has two garages on his property, and plenty of clean, well-lit space to store and work on his collection. This is the back garage, used more for storage, where some classic Fords reside along with more vintage signage. *Robert Genat*

"telephone booth cab" pickup, sliced and welded two sets of doors to make one set of longer ones, and added 10 inches to the back. For power he chose a Buick nailhead V-8. The truck was one of the first vehicles to come out of the So-Cal Speed Shop. Left coast fabricator and body man Steve Davis extended the body, while upholsterer-drag racer Tony "The Loner" Nancy did the interior.

De Heras likes hot rods, but he's not too hung up on particular manufacturers. Fords appeal because they have the best resale value and the widest parts selection. "Their design work was better than their assembly work," he finds, "but if you massage them, they're as nice as some of the bigger, more exotic cars." He likes to maintain the underlying vehicle's integrity by keeping such things as the original door handles and moldings. Under the hood, he'll stray a little further if it's an idea he likes—for example, the 1961 Ferrari V-12 lump he's putting in a '32 roadster. All of his hot rods are stick shift cars.

Horsepower Farm has a double meaning. The obvious one is the many sweet and swift moving vehicles on hand. The other goes to the origin of the term, real horses, which de Heras keeps and rides on his 35-acre property. *Robert Genat*

He has other four-wheeled prizes too, like a 1935 Cadillac Doctor's coupe with dual side-mounted spares—a rare feature. "Certain cars just appeal because of their design," he says, "something that has a really nice style to it." He cites the '57 Caddy and the '65 Riviera as examples.

De Heras is always on the lookout for a new project, too. "I always have three or four cars under construction." Another little number that should keep pace with fast company is a '55 Nomad that he's having fitted with Z06 Corvette running gear. Expect a 150-mile per hour car from that union. There will be others. All his cars get driven, and if there's one he doesn't drive—a car he doesn't bond with—he'll sell it to someone who might drive it. The same goes for a project in the works. If it doesn't seem like it's going to come together the way he envisioned, he'll cut it loose to make room for something else—something he'd rather set a wrench to.

This is a working garage with some nice accoutrements alongside the drill press and belt sander. Who wouldn't move a few tools and parts around to make room for a 1935 Cadillac and a rare aftermarket jukebox cabinet, fitted with Wurlitzer mechanism, from the 1930s? *Robert Genat*

Along with his cars, de Heras has one of the most complete collections of Wurlitzer jukeboxes in the country. He likes them not just for their history and music, but also for the ingenuity connecting buttons, records, speakers, and coin slots. *Robert Genat*

All of this activity gives de Heras a lot of time in his favorite place. He's not as skilled at blacksmithing, welding, and fabrication, but he does what he can. "I've had checkbook cars, where you have one shop do the work and just keep paying. That isn't how I like to do it." Where it's work he won't do himself, de Heras serves as a sort of general contractor. He finds the individuals he wants for particular jobs on the project and oversees the build. This gives him exactly the quality and style he wants, and, he says, it is often cheaper than having one shop do it all.

Regardless of whether others are building some of his projects, de Heras is always working on something too. "My garage is like my den," he says. "When the sun's out and I'm home, I'll be out there tinkering."

Except for the electrics, de Heras does all the jukebox restoration work himself. He's especially drawn to the early machines, with mechanisms representing the first efforts to coordinate accepting coins, registering selections, and getting a record playing. *Robert Genat*

In addition to jukeboxes, de Heras also collects coin-operated soda machines and related signs. Hang around the garage long enough, and you just might get a hankering for an ice-cold Coke. Maybe they're still a nickel. *Robert Genat*

The artwork on the walls relates to people de Heras has known and worked with or whose work or driving he admires. Some of it is signed by guys associated with the So-Cal Speed Shop, who worked on a few of de Heras' cars. His cars have been in 35 to 40 magazine articles in the United States, Europe, and Japan. *Robert Genat*

Don Audel

KEEPERS

Don Audel's "keepers" are his 'T Roadster and his wife of 45 years. Two of these cars are hers—the 1937 Ford flat-back sedan, with all powers and comforts and in her favorite color, aqua; and the Miata. When she told Audel she wanted a flame job on the Miata, he said it wasn't the right kind of car for that. But keepers have their influence. *Peter Vincent*

If your name is Don Audelovthelyotus, people will have a hard time remembering it—and you can forget about correct spelling. Shortened to Don Audel, it's not only easier to say, it's easier to fit on the side of your work truck, along with the words "& Son, Pinstriping." Now there's a name a lot of people know, because a lot of car and truck owners who want that little something extra in the finish have used his services.

Ask Audel how many cars he's pinstriped in his life and he'll tell you that's not the important part. What's much more meaningful to him are all the friends this work has brought him. It's also earned him a lot of respect and enough success to buy homes, nice hot rods, other cool autos, and an amazing collection of pedal cars. He isn't ducking the numbers question—he just can't answer it. Ask a doctor who's semi-retired how many patients he's treated and you'll probably get the same sort of response. Who could count?

Earlier in his career, Audel pinstriped over 1,000 cars a year. "That's for young people," he says. Today he works three days a week, pinstriping two or three cars a day. He was recently

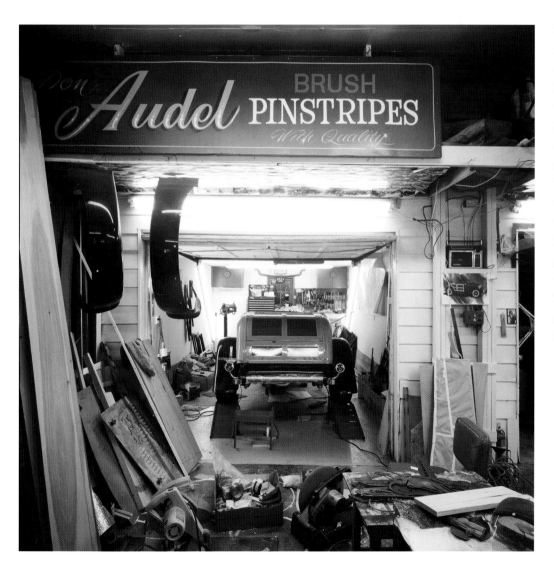

Ford never made a woodie roadster. Audel did. He started with a steel 1932 Ford cowl and a supply of white ash and mahogany. From there he cut every stick, steamed it, bent it, fitted it, and finished it. The completed handmade car won First in Class at the Oakland Roadster Show. The car is in the garage originally built with the house; on the back lot, Audel built an additional garage and studio space. *Peter Vincent*

This is the chassis that lies under the woodie roadster. Chromed axle and springs, plus modern, wide rubber leave no doubts that this is a hot rod. Audel knows how to fix cars, but he enjoys the build a lot more. "Hot rods are like sculptures," he says. Most enthusiasts, and virtually all hot rod fans, would agree. *Peter Vincent*

Absence makes the heart grow fonder with pedal cars, too. Audel was deprived of one as a child, but he's amassed a large collection to fill that void. Here's a sample of his 75 pedal cars, planes, boats, trucks, and tractors on display adjacent to his studio. *Peter Vincent*

up in Canada to do some antique cars, and he still does a steady stream of hot rods. He also works for a few car dealers and body shops—his regular fare.

We're not, of course, talking about the vinyl stripes you buy at Pep Boys and stick down the side of your car. No, Audel hand paints pinstripes with a fine brush in the traditional style going back to the early days of the automobile. He striped his first car when he was 13 years old. His buddy's uncle had a green 1941 Chevy and he wanted some pinstripes. Audel was the "school artist," so his name came up for the job. He took a whack at it and it turned out pretty good. And Audel enjoyed it.

Although he's done pinstriping work ever since, he didn't initially embark on that as a career. He was an art director for a large design shop for a while, and then served the same position for the 1974 World's Fair. "That was a real prestigious job," he says, "and you could look forward to getting sacked. World's Fairs don't last that long." Then his mom's boyfriend talked him into starting his own business. He focused on pinstriping and his brush hasn't been idle since.

"I've been a car nut since I was 12 or 13 years old," Audel says. Pinstriping has kept him in touch with that passion, and with other enthusiasts, his whole life. "I have a friend who used to build Indy cars, I have friends who are painters, body

Audel's vehicles often end up black, like this 1928 Ford Phaeton hot rod. He handmade many of the parts on these cars, which makes for a great custom look but proved a hassle when a young kid hit the 'T Roadster and destroyed the front end. Insurance paid to fix it, but Audel had to make many of the parts—again—because they were one-offs. *Peter Vincent*

A lot of designs and drawings have come out of this studio over the years. Audel was in art design before he became his own boss as a pinstriper. He continues to paint on canvass, design and build his own hot rods, and even carve birds out of wood. He used to illustrate calendars before the pinstriping business took off. This studio lies above the garage space he built on the back lot of his original house and garage.
Peter Vincent

men, machinists—all perfectionists," he notes. "Having the respect of people you respect really makes your life."

While pinstriping is his bread and butter, Audel's skills are broader. He loves to build hot rods and customs and lavishes the same attention on them that he does on his paint details. He built a 'T Roadster almost 50 years ago. He put it in a car show and brought an important young woman to see it on their first date. He still has the car and the woman—his wife of 45 years. "The 'T Roadster and my wife are my keepers," he quips. "They'll bury me in that car." Wouldn't be the first time an enthusiast took his own transportation to the pearly gates.

Though he doesn't build cars professionally, Audel puts enough care into them to win some prestigious honors. The 1929 Ford Sedan delivery he built over six years won the Model A Ford Club of America's nationals in 1981. He also won First in Class at the Oakland Roadster Show with his handmade 1932 woodie roadster—a car Ford never made. "Oakland's the Academy Awards of Hot Rod shows," Audel says. He'd been dreaming of that show since he was a kid.

At one time Audel had 27 cars, a few more than his wife felt were essential. He sold off a dozen to buy a house in Twin Lakes, Idaho, where he and his wife can sit out by the water and

Audel has said they'll bury him in his 'T Roadster, a car he built almost a half century ago, and rebuilt after a kid who'd had his license for two days hit it head on. What would Henry Ford say if he could see the creativity and craftsmanship hot rodders have lavished on the old Tin Lizzie? *Peter Vincent*

take a well earned break, or Audel can pick up a different brush and do a little watercolor painting—another of his pastimes. His garage and studio space abuts a house he used to own in Spokane, Washington. He sold that house, but kept the garage, along with his adjacent four-car garage with studio space above.

Audel believes his passions come in part from things he didn't have as a child. "I came from a poor family," he says. His Greek father never owned a car and never learned how to drive. Audel's half-century immersion in cars comes from wanting one so much as a kid. Another thing he longed for then, and has in abundance today, is pedal cars. He was looking forward to

inheriting his brother's pedal car for his birthday as a child. But when the day came that he was sure he would get it, he learned from his mother that she had given it to the fire department, which fixed them up and resold them. That disappointment may well explain his present collection of 75 pedal cars, pedal planes, and pedal boats—so many that he designed his house so they could hang on the walls.

The car scene also allows Audel to cross paths with old friends. In summer 2005, he ran into one of his first pin-striping mentors, Steve Pick, who showed Audel some tricks back in the early 1950s. Pick had his own chopped and

Sometimes when people can't quite understand what he has in mind, Audel will paint an image of his vision. Here he holds a watercolor of the woodie roadster, standing among the wood from which he crafted the body. *Peter Vincent*

channeled 3-window coupe when they were young and was someone Audel always admired. He did pinstriping for the local motorcycle shop. Watching him, Audel picked up the some of the fine points of the craft, which he's used and refined for five decades.

Living with cars, and in a sense through them, has given Audel many lifelong friends. He's still close with several of his buddies from the time he pinstriped his first car, and his work has brought him close to many, many more people. His wife is retired now, and he's semi-retired but it's hard to walk away. "You lay your life out and look at how much more you can expect to have," he explains. "We're on the short end of the dipstick, but I still can't give it up. I love what I do."

Audel follows a simple philosophy on life well lived: "I never had anybody come to my house to look at my stocks and bonds, but I've had lots of people who want to see my garage. It's your family and friends and the respect of your peers that make you rich."

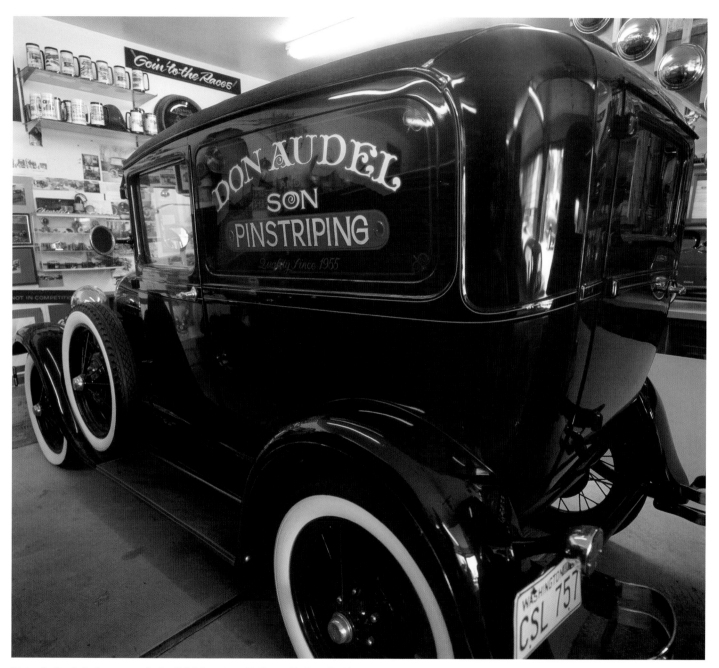

It took Audel six years to build his 1929 Deluxe Sedan Delivery, but it was good enough to win Best in Show at the 1981 Model A Ford Club of America nationals. When Audel's son—now a metal sculptor—was a kid, he used to accompany Audel and lay out designs for him. Ellis Island is responsible for shortening Audel's father's name from Audelovthelyotus, which would have required a longer truck. *Peter Vincent*

Vern Tardel

by Peter Vincent

STAYING AFTER OLD SCHOOL

Very nice chopped 1933 Ford five-window coupe. Authentic early hot rod power will come courtesy of the flathead engine in the foreground. The room at the very end on the right is the clean room set aside for engine building. *Peter Vincent*

I met Vern Tardel sometime in the 1990s through another friend of mine, Mike Bishop. Both were trying to get the Nash *Salt 'n' Peppers* blown, flathead-powered Bonneville race car ready for the awards ceremony at the Goodguys Pleasanton event. It was my first taste of the laid-back Tardel Traveling Circus. Tardel and company were very serious about what they were doing, but they also realized that racing should be fun and kept at a level that was real. They were not concerned with the one-upmanship that was so prevalent at that time in the hot rod and street rod culture. Their attitude made them some of the coolest guys on the block, which holds true to this day.

The next time I ran into Vern and the group was at Bonneville, where they were racing the Nash. Imagine a chopped 1951 Nash Ambassador, slammed on the ground with a 6-71 blower, injectors sticking out of the hood, and big red chili peppers painted on the side. These guys were always at Bonneville, and every year I got together with them out on the salt. The group grew, and saw the addition of Phil Linhares, the chief art curator for the Oakland Museum of California, and who owns a couple of cars crafted by Vern. Vern's accidental fame further spread when the San Francisco Museum of Modern Art (SFMOMA) Artists Gallery asked Linhares to curate an exhibit about hot rodding. The exhibition, which ran during fall 2002, focused on Tardel and his shop and set new attendance records.

Another view through Vern's shop showing various projects in different states and levels of finish. The helicopter rides are not available. *Peter Vincent*

Vern Tardel and Oakland Museum of California curator Philip Linhares with Phil's Tardel-built 1934 Ford four-door sedan. Renowned chassis builder, Kent Fuller, had a hand in reworking and creating some of the front sheet metal. *Peter Vincent*

This is the view you see when driving into Vern Tardel's shop area, showing a variety of hot rods in various states of finish. Some of these cars are full-on projects, while others came in for miscellaneous repairs and adjustments, or even just a visit. *Peter Vincent*

But Tardel is best known for his construction of early to mid-1950s-styled, flathead-powered hot rods, not his art gallery appearances. These are not modern replicas, but rather cars using original parts and 1950s building methods. Tardel's knowledge about early Ford parts and how they can be used and interchanged during the building process is well known throughout hot rodding, and his cars are as iconic as those built decades ago. Vern has been collecting vintage Ford parts for some 40 years, which has helped him stockpile all the bits necessary to build cars in his classic style. Hot rodding has come full circle, and Vern now finds himself at the center of what is the hot style of construction. He has the cars, the parts, and the historical and practical knowledge to build whatever he can imagine.

A walk through Vern's shop is a tour through hot rod history. Parts and memorabilia are everywhere. There are cars in different stages of build, as well as a few original cars stuck away here and there. It's a beautiful place that I have spent many an hour photographing and simply exploring. The shop is an education as well as a trip back to earlier times and forgotten ways. Life associated with these cars is just a little simpler, more mechanical, and direct.

No computer chips, power windows, or ABS braking on these cars. What you see is what you get, but you had better be able to work on them yourself, as they require tinkering and fussing over. They are hot rods of the most elemental variety, and you need to get intimate with them. Vern showed me a bone stock 1940 Ford sedan that he has had for many years. Sitting behind the wheel, I was transported back to my very first car. I was 15 again, and I was taking in everything—the smells, the feel, the sights—for just a few minutes. It was beautiful.

As the young men and women transfixed by hot rod culture in their youth matured, became successful, and began to build and collect the cars that first inspired them, hot rodding took off, reaching a prominence nearly on par with the most expensive limited production luxury and high-performance cars. Some hot rods use modern technology, but the classic style has really come into its own—exactly the type of car Vern has always loved and built.

Out on the Bonneville salt, we talked about the transition in the car scene and the point where Vern learned that his passion and profession had hit the mainstream. "One of the really amazing things that I noticed," Vern said, "—and I was unbelievably surprised it happened—is that these cars were accepted at Pebble Beach—the 1950s-styled hot rod. There was basically influence from some people that had cars way over and above hot rods, but they also liked the hot rods, so they allowed that particular kind of car in a concours. . . . I thought in no way in my lifetime would I ever see anything like that." Vern hadn't built any of these cars but they were done the right way, from his perspective.

Vern and Keith Tardel are standing behind David diFalco's roadster project. Keith has since opened his own very traditional hot rod shop, called Rex Rods, in Santa Rosa, California. *Peter Vincent*

"These cars are milestone cars in hot rodding," he said. "They are cars that were built by guys that were light years ahead of their hobby. They were perfectionists, and a lot of them at one point had been either in the aircraft industry, or had an engineering background. Some of these cars are absolutely done in the best possible way for their time."

Vern builds hot rods in the spirit of the cars that first turned him on—flathead-powered cars with early Ford running gear. He got the basis for his ideas the same place everybody else does—by poring over hot rod magazines. "[Drag racer and hot rod author] Don Montgomery was a very, very big influence in my idea to start doing these cars. I started looking for Montgomery stuff and looking at old photographs and picking out particular things in the photographs that I liked about the cars, particular features where somebody had taken a particular Ford part and done something to it,

This is a small view of the outside area and some of the vintage parts, which in this case are wheels as well as miscellaneous bodies waiting for current and future projects. There is a method to the storage, and a true order to it all. *Peter Vincent*

Michael McMillan, photographer David Perry, Peter Vincent, and Philip Linhares in Michael's "garage diorama" on opening night for the Real Hot Rods by Vern Tardel exhibit at the SFMOMA Artists Gallery in 2002. They even brought in the oil-stained carpets for authenticity. *Peter Vincent*

Another outside view toward the shop, through the flathead engine stack on the right and an old vintage Jeep on the left. If you are wondering, yes, it is a dry part of California. *Peter Vincent*

and enhanced the idea of the car. And having a really good strong background in the Ford V-8, and knowing the parts and interchangeability of the parts, I could spot what the person had done right off the bat. I could look at the photograph and say 'Okay, well that guy used the 1936 wishbone, or he did this or he did that,' so that basically gave me a real good platform to put these cars together, you know, and do them relatively inexpensively and in an expedient time frame. We're building one or two of these cars every four months."

In 40 years of hot rod building, Vern has amassed a deep inventory of parts and hardware to draw from. He is

well stocked in rear ends, transmissions, axles, springs, spindles, backing plates, steering gear pieces, headlight brackets, and old headlights that he buffs up. He doesn't have a freight yard full of original body parts and chassis members, but he looks for American stamped steel reproduction 1932 rails as a foundation. From there he builds his own center crossmember and uses stock front crossmembers or those from a particular pickup.

His target is a hot rod in the early postwar style, from 1946 to about 1956, made with genuine or proper reproduction parts from that era. One of the big differences between these cars and prewar rods is the rubber. "We've kind of veered away

Philip Linhares' 1934 Ford in Vern's shop with Pokey and Rusty, 2002. Note all of the memorabilia on the walls and the "clean restrooms" signs—cool stuff is everywhere. Vern's office is located behind Phil's sedan. *Peter Vincent*

from [prewar] tire combinations and put a lot of them on radials and 15-inch tires, which makes the car ride extremely well, but you lose the look of the very early, prewar stuff. But a lot of these guys are driving the shit out of these cars. I just drove one from Santa Rosa to Indianapolis, Indiana, and we put radials on it and it rode very nicely."

For Vern, each car he does is its own unique project. "I don't have a really strong formula for any particular car. Each one is kind of like a little art deal. It's like a little art show. And I don't say I have to put this headlight bracket on each one, because I don't have to. If I find something else that's really kind of cool, I'll screw that onto the damn thing."

Tardel has worked a long time perfecting his craft and his success is its own reward. It allows him to keep making the hot rods he loves, in the way he wants to build them.

Steve
Hamel

A FINE OBSESSION

Steve Hamel builds engines for owners far and wide—some for show, some for speed, some stock, some modified for power, or to accept electric start, modern alternators, or other improvements. The engine in the foreground is a show motor underway. The one toward the center of the shot is for a hot rod Vincent. *PixelPete*

Not every engine in the shop is a Vincent. The three toward the front of the shelf, with the diagonal sidecovers, are BSAs. Furthest left is an M21 600cc side-valve single from the early 1950s. To its right sits an overhead valve 500cc example. Above the box with the two curved tubes peaking out of it is a GB34 Goldstar motor—an early "big fin" version with oval flywheels to avoid piston interference. *PixelPete*

The World's Fastest Indian introduced a lot of moviegoers to a particular, thin slice of humanity determined to move fast— faster than anyone else on their vehicle type of choice—through their own courage, sweat, and ingenuity. Burt Munro, the main character in the film, was a real individual who set a record at the Bonneville Salt Flats that still stands. But Munro was not the only, or last, man of his type—the self-taught machinist, speed-dreamer biker hell-bent on making an old two-wheeled, piston-engined conveyance move like a modern supercar.

Steve Hamel, Minnesota motorcycle seller-turned-tuner, fuels his days with visions of the same intoxicating dash across that ancient level lakebed in northern Tooele County, Utah. While Munro's salt-burner of choice was a 1920 Indian Scout— modified continuously by the New Zealander over his years of record chasing—Hamel rides the venerated Vincent, likewise tweaked and tuned incessantly in search of a few more horse-power for a few more miles per hour.

Yet it wasn't Munro who inspired Hamel to tackle Bonneville's salt surface and the buffeting wind resistance that eventually stops any vehicle, no matter how powerful, from

Hamel spent two years building his speed record bike—no easy task but greatly aided when you have a full machine shop in your garage. Here its upper frame member rests on the Bridgeport milling machine. In Vincent's design, the engine is a stressed member and there is no down tube at the front of the bike. *PixelPete*

A 1951 Vincent Black Shadow motor (far right) shares a shelf with (moving to left) a 1950 Matchless G80 overhead valve single; a Moto Guzzi twin; a 1966 Triumph Bonneville; and a 750 Ducati. A reproduction safety sign reminds Hamel to exercise care here with the many machines that could make quick work of one or more fingers. *PixelPete*

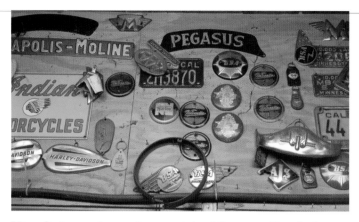

Manufacturers have always strived for appealing badges. In decades of selling, fixing, and modifying bikes, Hamel has collected many interesting emblems, which now form motorcycle art (or tractor art, in the case of the Minneapolis-Moline sign). The tin piece in the lower right is the original front-fender trim from his father's 1948 Harley Panhead, which got dented and replaced many years ago. *PixelPete*

Hamel's hero and target, Rollie Free, in his famous laid-out riding posture. Free is not in a bathing suit here. In these shots he's got a little skin protection in case he takes a tumble across the salt. The pinup calendar is from 1948, the year of Hamel's father's bike; the clock is from a Russian Yak-52 military trainer. *PixelPete*

accelerating. It was a previous motorcycle speed demon named Rollie Free, who hurled a Vincent across the flats in 1948 to a speed of 150 miles per hour. Free, in a bathing suit, laid on the bike, weight over the rear wheel, maximizing traction and minimizing his body's aerodynamic drag. "What Free did was superhuman," Hamel says. "It was comic book stuff. He immortalized Vincent." Free pushed his record to 156 miles per hour in 1950 and topped 160 for his fastest Bonneville run in 1953.

After Hamel heard about the amazing Rollie Free, he bought a Vincent in 1979. The foundation was laid, but he wouldn't set his own record for another 25 years. In the meantime he ran Sterling Cycle Works, selling Triumphs, Nortons, MotoGuzzis and Ducatis in St. Paul, Minnesota. "I had a lot of fun and lost a lot of money," he laughs. "I closed the shop in 1986, but my customers wouldn't leave me alone." Hamel bought property behind his old space and embarked on a post-retail life, fixing bikes. His shop is an old two-car garage, which he outfitted for motorcycle repair and

This is the downstairs of the house that accompanies Hamel's garage. When Hamel lived there, he had part of it set up as a Vincent museum. The table holds restored front and rear Vincent forks. A Harley Knucklehead motor stands in the window. The bike behind the Vincent with its wheel by a radial engine is a Seeley-framed Matchless G50. The radial engine came from a Travel Air biplane that crashed into a gas station in New Prague, Minnesota, in 1935. A farmer had the engine. Hamel bought it and is mocking up three cylinders' worth for a Morgan-style, front-engine car project. *PixelPete*

fabrication in 1990. "It's been the center of my universe ever since," he says.

Hamel's projects have evolved from fixing bikes to building more specialized—and fast—machines. Most of his work involves Vincents. He's building an engine for custom bike builder Matt Hotch that will go in a motorcycle Hotch is making for Discovery Channel's *Great Biker Build-off*. Hotch and competitor, Roger Goldhammer, will then run both of the finished bikes at Bonneville. Hamel's also building a Vincent race bike.

And he's always working and learning to increase his own speed at the salt flats. He already has a national record for a modified, pushrod gas bike with no streamlining. That's an American Motorcycle Association (AMA) record, as opposed to the Bonneville Speed Week Southern California Timing Association club records, but it's still the national best at 149 miles per hour. This record class requires the rider to sit upright, feet on the pegs—which is why this is a national record even though Rollie Free went faster lying down.

Three heads are better than one. To more than double the horsepower of the original engine, Hamel made a number of improvements, all to thousandth-of-an-inch precision. Dial indicators and a degree wheel help him set the valve timing for maximum speed. *PixelPete*

Conceptually, Hamel's record bike is a 1950 Vincent, but he's doubled the horsepower on that motor by tweaking it, mostly with new parts. He's making about 110 horses at the rear wheel, compared to a stock 1950 Vincent's 50 to 52 horsepower. An interesting facet of Bonneville record efforts is that horsepower isn't the major challenge—tire slip is. The engine doesn't get to max out its power against wind resistance because tire slip is the weak link. Get traction and you can flog the bike to a higher speed. "It's counterintuitive," Hamel says, "but at Bonneville you

want to be as heavy as possible." Rollie Free cheated the wind and tire slip by laying down over the back wheel of his bike.

Hamel thanks his dear, departed dad, Mel, for his motorcycle passion. "He had a '48 Harley panhead before I was born," Hamel recounts. "As far back as I can remember, I was sitting on the gas tank in front of Dad holding onto the gas caps on that Harley, smelling the gasoline, listening to the sound of the pipes, and feeling the wind in my face." The joy of those sensations has never left him.

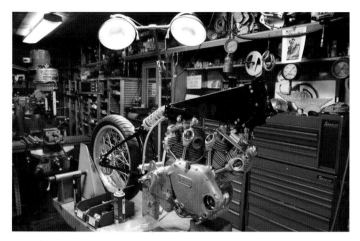

Building a half-century-old motorcycle to beat 150 miles per hour takes surgical care. This shot shows the engine's incorporation into the frame as a stressed member, with each cylinder attached to the upper frame, which also bolts to the original design's then-advanced mono-shock rear suspension. *PixelPete*

"I got my first motorcycle before I got my license," says Hamel, "a 1961 Triumph Cub. It came in pieces, and it's still in pieces." It's one of the projects many others have leapfrogged over the years. The first bike that he put miles on and rode, and broke, and fixed, was a 1967 CL 160 Honda "high pipe." It's one of the few bikes he's had that he doesn't still own. He has his father's Panhead, that first Cub, plus dozens of bikes by Triumph, Norton, BSA, Ducati, Velocette, and other manufacturers.

Many of those bikes could use a bit of wrenching too, but most will have to wait until a few more Bonneville records fall. Hamel has his heart and mind set on joining the 200-mile-per-hour club. He figures it will take him about five years to do it. He has to beat Rollie Free first—a mark he expects to achieve this year. The following year, he'll add some partial streamlining, which he projects will get him up near 180. Another year to increase power and refine his streamlining work should see him to 190, enough to surpass Munro's best of over 183, and then a further year with even more development to hit the magic double-century.

Vincent cam gears spread out for assessment. A digital camera is an excellent way to record any phase of a buildup or teardown for future reference. In the upper left is Hamel's Isle of Man TT record—LP record, that is. Steve and his wife, Wendy, took a motorcycle vacation to the Isle of Man, so the album is more than a gag. *PixelPete*

This view shows the big 42-mm Mikuni flat-slide carburetors on the Vincent Bonneville bike—so big, in fact, that Hamel had to notch the bottom side of the tank to accommodate the front one. It's the same carburetor as Japanese and Harley V-twins often run, according to Hamel. The difference is that those big bikes run a single example, whereas Hamel's Vincent breathes well enough to need two. *PixelPete*

A lot of learning, tire slip, and wind resistance stand between Hamel and another 50 miles per hour atop a 60-year-old motorcycle, but he welcomes the challenge. He lives for it. "Dad taught me basic mechanics. He was a child of the Depression. We were good at taking care of ourselves, taking care of our stuff, and not spending any money." He used his father's basic instruction and built on it to become a self-taught machinist, fabricator, and welder.

But breaking records takes more. To hit those speeds, Hamel says you need a network of specialists and tools, or you have to acquire what you need and learn how to use it. Hamel, who loves to fend for himself and find his own way, chose the second path. "You have to look for answers in unusual places," he advises. And he's not afraid to admit what he doesn't know and to seek guidance from anyone who might have fresh insights.

"When I started pursuing Bonneville, I had barely scratched the surface. Now I'm scratching deep," he says. He credits mentors who have been down the path he's on and shared their skills and knowledge. He is also very grateful to his wife, Wendy, for tolerating all his time in the shop, and for taking

On the night dedicated to getting the bike together and running, Hamel's friends turned out in strength to help make it happen, testing the electrical system, making safety checks, and sharing all their expertise and enthusiasm. Hamel ran the completed bike up and down the alley behind the garage once or twice and that was the only testing it got before he drove it faster than 150 miles per hour at Bonneville. *PixelPete*

Put a fast machine on Bonneville's seemingly endless flat surface and it's easy to understand why people come here from all over the world to see how fast they can go. Hamel and his Vincent set a record here and more will follow if Hamel has his way. *Stephen Doherty*

an interest in his passion. She has a 1969 Triumph Bonneville, which Hamel built for her, and a 1945 war department BSA M20, which she learned on. Not long after getting her license, she joined Hamel on her own bike for a two week tour on the Isle of Man. Their trip coincided with the Manx Grand Prix and an English vintage rally, for a motorcycle-intensive trip.

Burt Munro and Rollie Free are heroes to the small, driven cadre who make Bonneville the center of their world. Would

these legends be angry that challengers are gunning for them, seeking to knock them from the record books? Of course not, for they, more than anyone else, know the obsession that seizes men like Hamel.

Records, as they say, are made to be broken and for many of them, Bonneville is the final arbiter. Let the fastest man—or woman—win, and inspire another generation to be faster still.

MUSCLE CARS & THEN SOME

"Put it to a hundred-forty. If he catches us, I'll eat my Airedale."

— *Gary Busey* as *"Gibson"* in The Gumball Rally

Bill Goldberg

FROM GRIDIRON TO STREET IRON

Who wouldn't like to roll up to this stable at the end of a long day? When you're a kid, parking your Hot Wheels and Matchboxes at various angles and appreciating their great lines, how can you not dream of someday taking those cars to full scale—like this? *Robert Genat*

All power does not corrupt. At 6 feet 4 inches tall and 285 pounds, Bill Goldberg could throw a lot of men on their heads. In fact, he has done that, but only in a wrestling ring—and on a football field, and maybe a movie screen. Outside those venues, intimidating people is the last thing Goldberg wants. He'd much rather make someone smile or laugh, especially a kid looking to him as a role model.

The only power Goldberg is likely to throw around on the street is horsepower. Big-block, preferably four-speed; if it's a convertible, that's a plus too, though not essential. The first car he test drove was a 1970 Trans Am, and it made a big impression. His mother, who was with him, saw this and responded appropriately: "There's no way in hell I'm buying you this car." But Goldberg is not the type to let what he wants slip from his formidable grasp. He got a job and made decent grades, and his father helped him buy a 1976 model.

A Trans Am was an understandable goal for a high school student. In the longer term, Goldberg had bigger plans. His dream

Goldberg's '69 Dodge Charger R/T has the big-gun 426 Hemi powerplant. Overhead, exposed trusses lend a simple, architectural beauty to the garage space, and allow light to shine down from the windows above. *Robert Genat*

Neither England's AC company nor Carroll Shelby had a 6-foot 4-inch, 285-pound driver in mind when they designed the Ace and Cobra. So? The point of this car is to move, and with a NASCAR-grade Ernie Elliott motor, brother, it does. *Robert Genat*

was to play pro football, to be the best, to make a difference, and to give kids something to look up to. A pro sports career is a vision as alluring as a garage full of cars to many young men. For most, it is dream material only. Goldberg had the physical gifts and the discipline to make it real. He was a standout at the University of Georgia, and he won a spot with the Los Angeles Rams. From there he went to the Sacramento Surge of the

World Football League, whom he helped to win the championship World Bowl. He then returned to Georgia to don an Atlanta Falcons helmet.

Unfortunately, the metaphors we draw from sports and casually apply to more sedentary and less dangerous pursuits are the real deal on the gridiron. "Hit 'em hard" means hit them. Hard! "Throw yourself into it" means throw yourself into

your opponents, because these other very big, very powerful men—who have the same outstanding abilities that got you to the highest level of the sport—are going to slam you with everything they have. Waging turf war, Goldberg tore an abdominal muscle, an injury from which he could not rebound adequately to continue pro ball.

Trading pads for tights and stadium lighting for the pop and flash of a wrestling ring had never shared time in Goldberg's mind with visions of a Trans Am and a pro football jersey. But the NFL was out. Fate, for what it is, had some other plans.

Some top professional wrestlers trained at the gym where Goldberg worked out in Atlanta. They were friends, and they lobbied Goldberg to give it a try. He finally agreed. He trained for months and entered the ring against a 300-pound challenger, whom he pinned. Goldberg is frank that pro wrestling is part reality, part entertainment—"real wrestling" doesn't attract huge crowds. Still, when you lift a 250-pound guy over your head or slam down into the canvas, it's not special effects, and no stuntman subs in. He explains, "With football, you play sixteen games and travel six or seven times a season. You do that in three weeks in wrestling."

The wear and tear had a nice payoff, though. Fans loved it. Goldberg became a favorite from the get-go, and he rolled over— more accurately "speared and jackhammered"—an incredible

At the University of Georgia, Goldberg won all-SEC and All-American honors as guard. Those creds built the foundation for a pro football career with the Sacramento Surge and the Atlanta Falcons. *Robert Genat*

Another mover: '68 superstock Dodge Dart clone, which Goldberg built for SEMA. Famed superstock tuner Ray Barton put a 718-horsepower motor under the hood. A pair of air cleaners just visible through the scoop opening give away a dual-quad intake. *Robert Genat*

string of opponents in coining his trademark phrase, "Who's next?" He eventually took on and defeated Hollywood Hulk Hogan to become the WCW World Heavyweight Champion.

If the name on his paycheck has changed over time, his love of cars has not. One of fame and fortune's benefits is the ability to buy powerful cars. The concurrent need is to garage them. He has a few bikes and an alluring assortment of cars—about 17, but the number changes as he buys and sells. Horsepower is a consistent theme.

His garage started out as a 1,500-square-foot space with a kitchenette that had been converted to a little house and living area. The original owners' plan was to stay there while they built a house, but they sold to Goldberg first. He made it a four-car garage, then opened up the outer walls and attached an additional 5,000-square-foot garage area. The space is well lighted with ample access to the roads beyond—Goldberg likes to drive all of his cars, and a dozen garage doors make that easier.

"The cars are the stars of my garage," he says, and he's constantly moving them around, keeping them running, and making room for new acquisitions. Stacking is key to keeping it all housed—he has three Revolution lifts, with another two on order.

It's not a memorabilia garage. Though he collects sports items like helmets and jerseys, his automotive interests lie mainly in the machines themselves. He has an enviable batch of Mopars—four-speed Hemis prominent among them—but he's not a one-marque man. He has a Trans Am like the one he first test drove and a blown Boss 429 Mustang that's well storied and bitchin' fast. His quickest ride is a Cobra replica built by Ernie Elliot, Bill Elliot's brother, complete with Winston Cup motor (Ernie builds engines for NASCAR.) It'll pull the front end off the ground at 90. Some fast cars are a little small for Goldberg, but he's willing to put up with cramped quarters to wind out big power. Besides, a snug fit fends off the g forces.

The garage walls bear a few banners from companies whose products Goldberg likes, but most of the decor is not his doing. "My attention is centered elsewhere," he says. "Plus, I

There are a lot of Mopars in Goldberg's garage, but his preference is based more on style than brand loyalty. If it looks good and goes fast, there may be a space available. Here, Mopar clock has top billing over Chevy hood, yet hood bears the owner's face—so what does he like best? We're not going to argue with him over it. You go ahead. *Robert Genat*

don't have very good taste for what to put where." His wife, Wanda, has been a huge help in making it nice, with the paving stones, plants, and other ideas, like the styling of the open trusses and exposed beams. "She's an integral part of everything I do. It's wonderful to have a wife who's receptive to my love of all these things." Wanda has some passion for cars too—not surprising for

If this enticing 440-six pack 'Cuda coupe and convertible Hemi Challenger are putting some ideas into your head, consider the sign against the far wall: "Notice: Anyone found here at night will be found here in the morning." *Robert Genat*

Goldberg hosted a biker build-off that featured old school builder, Mondo. Goldberg's wife, Wanda, whose talents include being a blacksmith, farrier, and welder, was fascinated by Mondo's welding skills, so he gave her his signed helmet. Billy Gibbons, ZZ Top guitar player and big-time car guy, was on hand and signed it too. *Robert Genat*

You can't drive them all at once, which is good justification for adding a few on lifts and doubling your storage potential. A '68 Yenko Camaro and '67 Hemi Plymouth GTX make a desirable stack. *Robert Genat*

a professional stuntwoman—and is as eager as Goldberg to have their 1966 Jaguar E-type finished with its restoration.

Pro wrestling, like football, is now in his past, as the WCW folded at the height of Goldberg's popularity. But he stays busy. He still works out five days a week in a gym above part of his

garage space. On the reality show *Pros vs Joes*, Goldberg freestyle wrestled some tough characters. "I felt like the Joe," he quips, but the challengers were not better that day. Closer to his heart is his host gig for History Channel's *AutoManiac*, where he gets to drive amazing cars. Hollywood phones too,

Drag racer Al Eckstrand built two Lawman Mustang Boss 429s in conjunction with Ford. The cars were shown to U.S. servicemen to give them a taste of the muscle car scene back home, and maybe encourage a few sales. One of the cars was destroyed in a shipping accident. This is the second, beside the 1963 Dodge Candymatic drag car. The red and blue car is a '97 Thunderbird road course car Goldberg bought for track practice. *Robert Genat*

when scripts call for an imposing presence, as with his most recent role in *The Longest Yard.*

Yet it's little things that count more than what the public sees. Goldberg likes to visit hospitals and go to charity events for kids in very unfortunate situations. "For me it's the coolest thing in the world to put a smile on a kid's face," he says. Occasionally a kid is too shy even to look at him, but Goldberg doesn't drop this challenge either. Sometimes he'll toss the pen to the child and ask him for his autograph. Another grin won.

Jim & Gordon Wangers

THE GODFATHER, THE JUDGE, and THE CEO

The Wangers warehouse adjoins AMCI, the Wangers' company, which is best known for pioneering the competitive ride and drive events——where consumers get behind the wheel in a variety of environments——that are now commonplace throughout the industry. The open, brightly lit space houses their Pontiac fleet, plus an eclectic assortment of other vehicles. *Robert Genat*

If the country has gone nuts over muscle cars—and it has—Jim Wangers deserves some credit for helping muscle cars earn that name in the first place. The national drag racing champion and marketing guru was on the scene during the creation of the first GTO, and his ad copy put fire in youthful bellies to get hold of these street beasts and drop the hammer. His voice was in John DeLorean's ear, urging the Pontiac point man to give the public what they wanted: fast cars. He pushed Pontiacs throughout the muscle car era, and he still loves those larger-than-life machines.

The Wangers collection reflects Jim's pivotal years at Pontiac, but also his nephew Gordon Wangers' broader and more eclectic automotive tastes. Jim and Gordon share garage space as they have shared business objectives, working side-by-side at AMCI, an automotive marketing company that Jim started and Gordon joined shortly thereafter. AMCI was sold to advertising/marketing giant Omnicom in 2002. Gordon continues as CEO, while Jim devotes himself to "Godfather of the GTO" duties, attending national Pontiac enthusiast shows, races, and events. They keep about 20 cars on hand in a 6,000-square-foot space adjoining their business offices.

Gordon's collection runs from a 1936 Rolls Royce to a 1970 Can-Am race car. The McLaren is one of the fastest small-block vintage race cars in its class. He usually runs a 355 Chevy in it, but he's thinking about swapping in a 427 small block (not big block) for even more juice. *Robert Genat*

Jim is known in enthusiast circles as the godfather of the GTO. His favorite of all of them is the 1969 Judge, of which he has two—this one on the left coast and another in Detroit for use around the Motor City. The Ferrari 360 Modena is Gordon's and wears unusual "grigio" paint color. *Robert Genat*

Jim's "absolute favorite GTO, without exception," is the Judge. As a key figure at Pontiac's ad agency, he was on DeLorean's committee that developed the Judge concept. They wanted to stay ahead of the tastes of young people in the mid-to-late-1960s. "The car was sort of a spoof of itself," Jim reflects. "Muscle cars had matured significantly, and there was only so much more you could do with these pieces of sheet metal hung on running gear that was under-braked, overweight, and overpowered." They couldn't change the underlying car, whose specs were corralled by GM, so they had to change the look.

"Look!" was what the resulting styling commanded. With its pop art decals, grotesque stand-up blade spoiler (mild by today's standards but off the design charts in 1969) and solar flare orange paint, the Judge grabbed eyes that had never discerned one car from another. "We created an outrageous package," Jim recalls, and it was a huge success. The smartest thing they did, he adds, was to make only two engines available for the Judge—high performance and higher performance. This ensured that every Judge on the street packed a wallop.

Jim was present with John DeLorean and other key Pontiac players when they hashed out the '69 Judge. The car pushed boundaries outside with its over-the-top appearance as well as under the hood, where buyers could only choose between the GTO's two most powerful engines. *Robert Genat*

The story of the name is well known. DeLorean was an enthusiastic TV watcher and he liked the show Laugh-In. One of its comic bits involved the chant, "Here come da judge." So DeLorean said, let's give them the Judge. The name had pop-culture cred, but a broader clout too—as the arbiter of right and wrong, or in the street world, fast or slow, Judge was an author-itative name—an entity not to be messed with.

Of this, his favorite GTO, Jim has two examples—both '69s, of course. He was against carrying over the Judge concept to the 1970 model year. He felt the car was more a promotion for fast

Pontiacs than a stand-alone model. It had served that purpose very well and should therefore be retired before it went stale. But others in the organization wanted to keep on with a good thing. They changed the styling, painted it white and called the car the Humbler. "Except in white the car was kind of a nothing," Wangers says. "The '70 got welded to the showroom floor."

The committee that developed the original Judge called an emergency meeting in December 1969 to decide what to do. They concluded that what made the first Judge hot, above all else, was its paint. Problem was, the restyled car didn't look good in

Above Jim's '66 GTO and Gordon's '65 Malibu hangs a poster of a commemorative stamp produced by one of Jim's friends, Art Fitzpatrick. "Fitz," as Jim calls him, painted the cars in Pontiac ad art during the "wide-track" era, 1959–1971. *Robert Genat*

Art and memorabilia make up only a small part of the Wangers collection. One piece Gordon told himself he would someday have, when circumstances permitted, was an original Alfredo De La Maria painting of a 1950s-era grand prix race. He now owns two. *Robert Genat*

Carousel Red, the obviously orange color that had popped the '69 into a new visual dimension. The '70 car was longer and somehow, with its Frenched headlights, it looked distasteful in the same shade. They called the original supplier and got a different hue, Orbit Orange, and that, Jim says, sort of rescued the '70 version.

During his Pontiac years, Jim had several cars every year to drive. But he didn't hold onto any of his original GTOs. Those in his collection now are cars he's acquired since, examples of cars that meant something to him. They're years he likes but

not the exact cars whose memories sparked the purchases. The one he wished he hadn't sold was the original GTO that *Car & Driver* reviewed when Pontiac first released the car in 1964. It was a car spec'd to move, and it did, putting Pontiac's new offering in a very good light.

Jim had the car, but he let it go, selling to a Detroit area police officer who had been generous to him in the matter of speeding tickets, something the former drag racer was good at attracting. The officer held onto that '64 for the rest of his life,

Besides highlighting the occasional car show win, silver cups yield interesting reflections—in this case the garage's checkerboard floor. The ribbons were won by a Delahaye 135M with Figoni and Falaschi bodywork; the Delahaye is no longer in the collection. *Robert Genat*

Like the Judge of the same year, the '69 Trans Am featured Pontiac's functional Ram-air intake for some extra horses. Jim says, despite equal power, the Judge with its wild paint and details drew much more attention than the Trans Am on the showroom floor. *Robert Genat*

and his widow sold it before Jim got wind of the sale. The next owner turned it over a few years ago for many times his purchase price. If Jim can't have it, he at least likes its current owner—the son of one of Jim's Detroit colleagues. Jim had given the son a spirited ride in the car some 35 years before. Afterward, the boy told himself that one day, he would own that car. He did his homework, like a good kid, and now he does.

Jim's collection includes other hot Pontiacs too, especially Trans Ams. He has a '69, '79, '89, and '99, all "anniversary"

cars—the best examples of each generation, in his eyes. He also built a modern tribute to the famous GeeTO Tiger, which was actually two GTOs that company reps would bring to the drag strip in the mid-1960s. They traveled with a driver in a Tiger suit, who would race individuals from the crowd in whichever car the lucky fan didn't pick. Jim's car is built with a proper body, salvaged from a bone yard, but with a conglomeration of modern speed parts. While the original cars ran 12.90 for the quarter-mile, according to Jim, the modern replica does 10.70.

The commercial building housing the Wangers cars offers plenty of ceiling clearance for lifts, should stacking ever become necessary. Big block Camaro SS was a Trans Am rival in its day, while Gordon's '59 Caddy—an Eldorado Biarritz convertible—is an icon of the previous decade. *Robert Genat*

Jim pitched Pontiac the idea of reprising the GeeTO concept, this time pitting his updated tribute car against the new generation GTO. It seemed like a great way to lure back the crowd that made the model successful to begin with. Pontiac balked, though, and squandered what Jim felt was a nice opportunity. That won't stop him from enjoying his car—or any fast Pontiac.

Nephew Gordon looks anywhere and everywhere in his automobile hunt. "I have no rhyme or reason to my purchases," he says. "I buy whatever strikes my fancy." The resulting accumulation covers some 70 years and manufacturers from Chevy to Ferrari, from Holden to Rolls-Royce.

The Rolls was a present to himself, bought at Christmastime, but only incidentally. "I had a good year at AMCI and it was Christmas Day. I'm Jewish, so I didn't have anything to do. I was surfing the 'net with money burning a hole in my pocket." He stumbled on a car that a dealer in nearby Thousand Oaks had sitting on the lot. It was represented as ready to drive on rallies, an idea Gordon liked. He sent an area Rolls expert to have a look and see if the car was worth buying. The answer came back yes.

Jim Butler Performance pushed Jim's GeeTO Tiger's 400-cubic-inch engine out to 467 cubes for a 2-second improvement over the original car in the quarter-mile. *Robert Genat*

"Two and a half years and $38,000 later, it now runs," jokes Gordon. He doesn't feel taken. The car drives well, and his research has revealed that it's the only 1936 Rolls-Royce Phantom III Barker Coupe in the world.

How different this refined road car is from his 1970 McLaren M8C Can-Am race car. He says it's the first- or second-fastest small-block vintage racer of its class in the country. "It's won every vintage race that hasn't had a big-block car." This is the one vehicle in the Wangers collection that isn't road driven, but Gordon gets behind the wheel when it isn't a major contest—when it is, pro Tim Gaffney takes the controls.

Gordon's had the McLaren up to 170 miles per hour, about 10 shy of its top speed. That's fast enough. "You have to have some respect for it," he says. "It's a pretty dangerous car"—mostly because of its 1970 technology. "Your feet are out in front, there's a little roll bar, and no safety cage."

Other fast toys include a 1,000-horsepower 1965 Malibu resto-mod street/strip car. This Chevy is street driven and hasn't hit the drag strip, though Gordon has crunched the numbers and believes it could run an eight-second quarter off its leash.

Jim, who turns 80 in 2006, is winding down his national event touring, but he'll keep enjoying his fast iron and no doubt will stay active in the marketing business. And if a certain 1964 GTO comes available, those drag-racer reflexes will cut loose with a pen and a checkbook, signing off in record ET.

Other cars will join the collection too, when Gordon gets the itch and the right machine—one he may not anticipate—captures his attention.

Jim's tribute to the GeeTO Tiger, a Pontiac promotion played out at drag strips, takes advantage of modern performance components like four-wheel disk brakes, but retains its period look. *Robert Genat*

Julian Balme

LONDON CALLING— FORD, TOO

A perfect storage and tinker space near the heart of London. Only the Spitfire has no Ford connection, though at least it's black—like the Galaxie is and the Tiger will be. It's actually one of the few Spitfires to come in black, a color Balme's mother special ordered from the factory. *James Mann*

To the man in rural Iowa, a few garage stalls with shop space attached may not feel like the find of the century. Julian Balme is not an Iowan. His garage lies in one of the most populous cities in the world—an international commercial center for almost two thousand years. Unless your name has "King" somewhere near the front of it, you won't be putting up a 10-car pole barn in central London anytime soon. This is a dream garage, Old World style.

It's fitting that Balme should own this plot, as he's good at being in the right place. That knack accounts for the fact that a lot of us know Balme. We might not pick him out on the sidewalk, but we're familiar with his work. For example, if you read *Classic & Sports Car* magazine, you've probably seen his Ford Falcon Sprint, white with a blue top and nose stripe, snarling

The English issue of *Esquire* magazine did a feature on the best getaway cars, which included Balme's Galaxie. The man at the wheel is not Clive Owen, from the BMW getaway films, but an even faster driver—Formula 1 World Champion Damon Hill. *James Mann*

A "plan chest" is a more traditional way to store an artist's work, but Balme didn't want to take up the space for his portfolio. Instead, the posters and photos make a great backdrop for cool cars. *James Mann*

The lift the Lincoln's sitting on makes underside work on any of the cars a lot easier. The engine beneath the bell housing on the floor is a Super Cobra Jet 428 destined for the "gasser" project. It came from a kit Cobra that ran 11-second quarters on street tires, so it should move things along. *James Mann*

The '54 Lincoln shot at the Bonneville Salt Flats. Balme didn't get registered in time to run the car, but the event was still a blast. For the Carrera Panamericana, which he drove with Mick Walsh, Balme used a Spanish version for his name. *James Mann*

and scrabbling across its pages. Balme the driver campaigns the Falcon in every cool venue that will open its gates to him.

If you've never read *C&SC* (what sort of car fan are you, anyway?), you may still recognize Balme's work. Anyone who turned on a radio or walked into a music store in the 1980s knows the British punk band, the Clash. Balme the graphic artist designed the covers for their albums *Sandinista* and *Combat Rock*. Before that, he did album art for Adam Ant, another big name in the British music scene from the early days of MTV.

Balme has always been into art, and he's always been into cars. Success in the one has led to a lot of fun in the other. The music story goes like this. Balme had a band-focused fanzine in college. He met his friend, Kosmo Vinyl, at a couple of shows, and then Kosmo helped Balme out with his publication. Kosmo worked in the music industry and connected Balme with the Clash when the emerging punk band needed designs for its album covers. Balme was in the right place, already doing work for the Clash's label, CBS, and for Stiff Records, whose offices were next door to the Clash's management.

He didn't know the band personally, but he did get in on some of the scene around their shows. "The first time I met Joe Strummer, he was telling the night watchman at his hotel that I was his brother-in-law to get me into the party in their rooms." Strummer (writer, vocals, guitar), was also a big fan of Balme's black Ford Galaxie. The Clash called it quits about the same time Balme was growing tired of the music scene. He decided it was time to indulge his interest in cars.

California black plate means a lot to collectors in the United States. Despite the Lincoln's being registered in England, Balme's attention to detail keeps it a uniquely American car. *James Mann*

Balme and some collected items. The photo over his shoulder shows the Falcon attacking Lord March's lawn on his way to winning the Monte Carlo Rally class at the 2001 Goodwood Festival of Speed. *James Mann*

A few more knickknacks to decorate the walls. Balme and his wife have spent a lot of time driving around the United States, often in one of Balme's cars and usually to spots with an automotive focus. *James Mann*

The theme for the Balme collection is Ford. His youthful fantasies were filled with the Cobra, Shelby's Ford-powered sports car milestone. That was beyond budget though, so Balme found himself a Sunbeam Tiger, a less expensive way to get British styling wrapped around a Ford V-8. He first built up the car as a replica of the Doane Spencer Hollywood Sports Car Tiger of the mid-1960s, which gave more expensive and refined Corvettes and Jaguars a hard fight on U.S. race tracks in SCCA B production.

Balme raced his too and caught the attention of *Classic & Sports Car* editor Mick Walsh. Balme was in his late 20s at the time, and Walsh liked the pluck of this young driver taking on older and better-financed competitors. Balme also cut a rebel image competing in a leather jacket, but he'd only thrown that on, he says, "because it was pissing down with rain" when he left for the race. Walsh did a story on the young racer. After the interview, he told Balme, "If you can write like you

What is and what will be. The Tiger was originally built like the Doane Spencer Hollywood Sports Car Tiger. Spencer got a lot of speed out of what was originally an inexpensive car. On the wall is a blow up of Balme's last race with the car before he embarked on a much needed body restoration. *James Mann*

talk, you ought to write some stuff for us." He's been contributing pieces ever since.

Next car on his mind was a GT350, but his shopping list was still ahead of his bank account. Instead, he bought the Falcon Sprint, which has paid him back many times over in fast laps and grins. "That car's always looked after me," he says.

He's had it at Laguna Seca in California, Spa in Belgium three or four times, the old Nurburgring racetrack in Germany, Monza in Italy, and the Goodwood Festival of Speed and Revival Meetings in his home country. When Ford had its centenary in 2003 at Dearborn, Balme showed up in the Falcon—the only car registered in England to attend.

In addition to the Falcon and its larger sibling, the Galaxie, which has done some rallying and nostalgic drag racing, Balme also has a 1954 Lincoln. He found the car behind an upholstery shop on his way to Las Vegas during one of his U.S. visits. "The owner had rechromed the front and rear bumper and taken it for reupholstery," Balme says, "but the car needed everything." He had the body and mechanicals redone, and then kept it in the United States for 10 years.

The Lincoln saw much use from Atlantic to Pacific. In one trip, for example, he and his wife had come over for the Monterey Historics. He then learned that the featured car at Pebble Beach was Lincoln, so they drove there, then to Reno, then Bonneville, Steamboat Springs, Yellowstone, Pikes Peak, Detroit, and then New York state to go to Watkins Glen.

A bigger test for the Lincoln was the Carrera Panamericana, the coast-to-coast race in Mexico reserved to cars built from 1940 to 1954. The Lincoln handled 7,000 miles in that journey without incident. The only failing was the dash lights, which crapped out in the first mile of the trip—a very small price to pay. "I've always been really, really lucky with that car," Balme notes. He calls it "the magic car." It's only let him down once, in Reno, in the forecourt of the Flamingo Hotel. But Balme was in the right place again: hotel staff said there was a 1950s Mercury specialist just up the street—probably the only place of its sort in the state, if not the country. The car went off to the 1950s expert, and Balme and his wife checked out the Harrah's car museum.

His other Fords include an Anglia grocery-getter and parts runner, and a '57 two-door ranch wagon "gasser" project. The Anglia's lucky it's a Ford. "I've come close to setting it on fire, because it's so unreliable," Balme laughs. The gasser project has a comic aspect too. He bought it on eBay for 500 bucks. "It

Though he wanted a GT350, Balme's gotten amazing service from the Falcon. Think he chose the blue and white paint scheme as a nod to the Shelby Mustang's most common livery? *James Mann*

The Galaxie only had two hub caps when it arrived in the United Kingdom, so the wheels were quickly upgraded to American Racing Equipment Torque Thrust Ds. As for the poster—the King of Rock 'n Roll, Vegas in the 1960s, motor racing, AND Ann Margaret—what more does a man need? *James Mann*

was built in 1970 by three complete animals in Kansas," Balme explains. "You wouldn't want to meet them at night, judging by their abuse of this car. It must have been the scariest, nastiest ride anyone could be put in." That car's

off getting the bottom two inches or so replaced from front to stern so it can handle a 428 engine.

There's a Lotus Elan 2+2 in the collection as well, which fits because it runs an English Ford-based engine. Only

Balme's garage includes a workshop area. It's wired for sound of course, and includes a turntable. What would you expect from a man who has designed many album covers? *James Mann*

the Triumph Spitfire has no Ford connection and remains, so far, attached only by emotional ties. The car was his mother's, ordered new, and Balme inherited it when she passed away. He'd always planned to sell it and buy a 1930 Ford Model A, but it's proven harder to give up than he thought—though not for any automotive reason. "It's the most uncomfortable car I've ever driven in my life," he complains. "My backside goes

to sleep within 10 minutes." Somewhere his mother's probably laughing at that—a little sacrifice in her memory.

Balme has no modern cars. "They scare the crap out of me. I open the bonnet and I only recognize two things, the washer bottle and the dipstick." Might help if it said "Ford" somewhere prominent, but then Balme doesn't need a modern car. He only drives on weekends anyway—and that's the beauty of a garage in central London.

A TASTE FOR SPORTS CARS

"It is no mere cynicism that 'nobody remembers who came in second' and the cars we remember best are the ones that won races."

— *Colin Campbell*, The Sports Car: Its Design and Performance

Henry Pearman

A LOVE FOR THE "E" AND GROUP C

An airy second floor provides space to relax and meet with Eagle customers, as well as a view of the E-types inside and the surrounding woodlands. To the left is where the new E-type bodyshells are prepared. *James Mann*

Henry Pearman has the E-type in his vanes. It's a silhouette as unmistakable today as when the car was first introduced almost a half-century ago. *James Mann*

Few people on earth have a legitimate reason for disliking the Jaguar E-type. What's legitimate? It's too beautiful? Too sexy? Too provocative? You don't like leather? Allergic to cats? Not liking E-types has a whiff of the disingenuous, like hating sunny days, or perfect beaches, or eating up a stretch of country road in a car born to run with the wind in your hair and your best gal at your side.

Apart from the curmudgeons, the fibbers, the born contrarians, there are really only two camps: those who love Jaguar's iconic creation, and those who love it very, very much. The first crowd will follow an E-type with their eyes till it disappears from view. The second would hawk a house, a farm, a kidney, or the rest of the family for a chance to own one. There is no such thing as an E-type fanatic, because any level of infatuation seems reasonable. With one of these cats held fast in your garage, how bad could life be?

Henry Pearman got the E-type bug at age three or four, the first time he saw one. "It's the car that pressed all the right buttons," he says. It wasn't the first car he owned—that was a Mark I MG Midget, which he bought for £25 when he was 15 years old. He managed his first E-type at age 18. It was a genuine basket case, collected in boxes. Things have improved.

Today Pearman's E-type collection of about 45 cars is the largest in the world, and his devotion to Coventry's cat is second to none. Where the average admirer is content with a design that was well ahead of its time and can still keep pace with all but a few modern cars, Pearman wants today's E-type to be every bit the standout performer it was in 1961, when the out-of-the-box 150-mile-per-hour production Jaguar introduced a new sports car era. If that means rebuilding every system

The main barn-style garage holds about 30 E-types. Pearman has two or three of each model throughout the years, though no two are identical in specs. The buildings were once part of a small farm in the heart of Sussex. *James Mann*

The collection includes the car Pearman drove to victory in the 1989 Pirelli Classic Rally, which he has owned since 1987. The car was prepared for the contest but he made no special modifications. It now serves as a test bed for Eagle's upgrades. *James Mann*

As a lifelong fan, Pearman has seen almost every kind of E-type collectible. The trophy cabinet contents date back to 1979, when he first took out a little time for competition, at 16 years old, competing for "Young Driver of the Year." *James Mann*

and part to like-new condition, fair enough. Yet Pearman will take performance enhancement as far as an owner wants to go, retaining the looks and spirit of the original design, but raising suspension and powertrain potential into the modern supercar realm.

You may ask why. Because he believes anyone who loves this remarkable car should be able to drive it today with the same confidence and prowess that the car bestowed off original showroom floors and racetrack starting lines.

If you like E-types, read sports car magazines, or visit any of the big car events in Britain, you've heard of Eagle E-Types, (eaglegb.com) which Pearman established in 1984. He's been rebuilding E-types to better-than-new standards since 1993. You might even think it's a big-volume operation and that dozens of Eagle Jags hit the streets each year. In fact, annual output averages just two cars, with a waiting list of three to five years. They've just signed on car number 28, due for completion in late 2008.

Pearman's garage lies in the heart of Sussex on a 15-acre plot surrounded by 100 acres of woodland. It doubles as the Eagle showroom, which sells between 30 and 40 E-types a year, but E-types aren't the only cars on the premises. Another obsession seized Pearman in the early 1980s. That's when he went to a talk by five-time Le Mans winner, Derek Bell. Shortly afterward, he watched his

The E-type collection spills into this side garage. Car 86 PJ, driven by Roy Salvadori and restored by Eagle, is one of the original 12 "lightweight" racers built with aluminum bodies and engines to battle Ferrari. It sits next to an Eagle E-Type lightweight. On the left is the Formula 1 Benetton in which Michael Schumacher scored his first two podium finishes, in 1992. *James Mann*

Much of the Group C collection is linked in some way to driver Derek Bell, who raced for the Rothmans Porsche team. One of the Rothmans cars in the collection led in the first Le Mans 24-hour race Pearman visited, in 1983. That car is pictured here, behind Rothmans Porsche chassis Number 1. *James Mann*

first Group C sports car race from the pits at Brands Hatch. Pearman had an internship at the track as part of his schooling in motor industry management. The Group C class limited the amount of fuel each car could use for the race, but allowed a wide variety of engines, and thereby manufacturers. Speeds surpassed 200 miles per hour—handily by the end of the series. The power and speed of these cars, their elegant and innovative designs, and their drivers' skills gave Pearman a new focus. He wanted a Group C racer.

Today, the Group C collection stands at about 18 cars. "Half or two-thirds of those cars are linked to Derek Bell or his

career," Pearman says. He's gotten to know Bell over the years, and the legend has promised to drive Pearman's cars in historic races. The jewels in the collection:

· the Miller Porsche 962, in which Derek won his last 24-hour race, at Daytona, in 1989;

· the Shell Dunlop works Le Mans entry for 1988—the last works Porsche entry, which finished second at Le Mans, after appearing set for a win and finishing on the same lap as the winning Jaguar;

· the first works Rothmans car built, Porsche chassis

956-001, in which Derek won the Group C class on the car's world debut at Silverstone in 1982.

"One day, I'd love to get a Le Mans winner," Pearman says; "I take the view that if I'm meant to have one, hopefully it'll come. I had tried to buy my first Silk Cut Jaguar in 1989, whilst at Le Mans, and had to wait until 1999 to finally achieve my ambition!"

Though he's modest about his own driving skills, Pearman knows how to handle the cars he collects. He won the Pirelli Classic Rally in an E-type in 1989, besting a field of challengers that included Stirling Moss and Timo Makinen, over a week's driving covering some of Europe's most challenging terrain. He has also taken the checkered flag at the wheel of a Group C car, winning his debut event in his own Jaguar XJR-11 in a revival race in 2002. Of course it didn't hurt that he was codriving with Win Percy, three-time British Touring Car Champion and two-time winner of the Spa 24-hour race. "He gave me the car with a 17-second lead," Pearman points out, but his own effort was a bit harrowing: Pearman's foot got trapped by a cable used to adjust the brake pedal,

Jaguar sports car collectibles include much from the Group C side. Le Mans is a favorite venue for Pearman, and this case includes two of the trophies from that track for 1988 and 1990, both awarded to the winning Jaguar. *James Mann*

Pearman with two of his Group C cars. He also collects memorabilia, including drivers' suits, mechanics' "set-up pages" for the cars, qualifying sheets, finisher's medals, and anything else he can get his hands on. *James Mann*

Another extensive piece of the Group C collection is miniatures. Pearman would love to get all the cars and liveries, but that's an ambitious goal, he admits. The top row is just one car, which ran in at least six different liveries, over just two seasons. *James Mann*

and he couldn't do much braking—helps keep your speed up, and your adrenaline.

There was a time when Pearman might have pursued a serious racing career, but he left that path to run Eagle and to follow his earliest passion, the E-type. He retains the same love and reverence for the car that he always had, and any number of attributes can make one special. He has had some of the earliest E-types made, and one of the last; he has restored one of the original lightweight racers, and built a "continuation" lightweight to original specs. Finding a well-preserved one-owner E-type is as thrilling as getting one owned by a big star, like soccer great George Best, whose fixed-head coupe was once part of the collection. A particular honor is that Eagle is entrusted to care for the very first E-type—77 RW—for the Jaguar company.

He also seeks out cars from his own past. Early in his career, a friend hired him to help set up a Ferrari dealership by buying cars, but Pearman's first purchase for the company was an E-type! What else would you expect of a man with leaping cats in his pupils? The car showed only 21,000 miles and came to the dealership for £6,000.

When the Silk Cut Jaguars first appeared in 1986, Jaguar became a more serious contender, dominating the series the following year, and going on to win Le Mans in 1988. The sole car from the 1986 Le Mans team was one of Pearman's early purchases for that branch of his collection. It now sits below the library area with the E-types. *James Mann*

All of the Group C cars run. Pearman says the Porsches, in particular, are amazing for practicality—"Any competent road driver could drive one." And no doubt would like to. They even have an all synchromesh road-car-style gearbox. *James Mann*

Pearman bought the same car for his own collection in 2006. The beauty of running Eagle is that Pearman gets to do professionally what he would do regardless—hunt for the best E-types.

He'll continue to move Eagle forward, keeping pace with innovations that make the car as good as it can be without diluting the spirit of the original. Yet he expects no significant production increase. "We may get to 2 1/2 or 3 cars a year, and that's where it will end," he says. "We like to live the passion of every car we build—it's taken us over 20 years of pure focus to do it." Pearman sums up that passion with a simple image. "You can jump out of the latest sports saloon or exotica, get into an E-type and come back with a huge smile."

Jon Shirley

RESTORE IT, SHOW IT—DRIVE IT!

In addition to this well-lit assortment of some of the world's great automobiles, the Shirleys also possess a large collection of Ferrari literature—one of the biggest in private hands. Preserving that history is as important in some ways as preserving the cars themselves, for there are few Ferraris to own, but there are many people interested in fine sports cars. *David Gooley*

Along with about 30 full-size cars, the Shirley collection also includes models of every Formula 1 Ferrari and most of the cars outside Formula 1. This showcase also features some interesting parts, such as race wheels and engine components, which came off the collection's cars during restoration work. *David Gooley*

How does the automobile, a machine like uncountable others, inspire so much passion? It is metal, it is leather, it is glass. Gears, nuts, bolts. Oil and gasoline. Why can this object grab your eye? Stop your breath? Quicken your pulse? Cause you to run down the street, or follow a lead half-way around the world? How does a collection of inanimate parts, assembled just so,

Modern Ferraris are welcome too, such as this F355, though Jon finds that he usually gravitates to the older cars when it's time for a spin. For a change of pace, his Mercedes 300SL Gullwing and roadster offer ample driving pleasure. Beside them, Ferrari's 512 Berlinetta Boxer was a regularly featured supercar with the magazines during its production years. *David Gooley*

No Ferraris are sold here, but the company certainly benefits from having a sign over such an outstanding collection. The hungry and curvaceous 1950s front end embodies some of the design cues that make cars of the period so striking. *David Gooley*

The ex-Schumacher car is probably the fastest in the collection, but any of these race cars would offer ample excitement. The other open-wheel car is a 1969 F-312. The Ricci car is a 1953 375 MM and the number 14 car beside it is a 1956 290 MM. *David Gooley*

stir such excitement that men and women will alter their lives, shape their dreams, plan their futures around possessing or driving this one machine?

Cars speak. Running or still, they speak to our ears and they speak to our souls. Everything we can be at our best, a car can be, too. Fast, agile, sexy, alluring, powerful, an object of desire or fear, a winner, a star. They speak with their lines, their performance, their tally of wins. They speak with their engines:

"Get in."

"Get over."

"—Goodbye."

Jon Shirley has a wonderful collection and he knows how to enjoy it—restoring cars when they need it, showing them at their best, then driving them on the roads and the race courses in the manner in which they were built to be driven. *David Gooley*

Above this automotive cacophony, one voice arguably rises above all others: Ferrari. It is the one renowned marque in the world for which the specific model is almost irrelevant. When someone says he has a Ferrari, you want to see it. You want to hear it. You want to take to the roads and show them why they were made—to awaken the senses. Ferrari builds cars to make hearts race and souls soar.

And Jon Shirley knows it. He had some Ferraris before, but when he retired in 1990, he decided it was "time to get involved." His timing was good, as the car market had slumped. Incredible cars were available for tantalizing prices.

Not all the cars he has collected bear the prancing horse. There were others that had made an impression on him, or that he had owned, which he sought out again. But Ferrari became a special pursuit. He and his wife, Mary, have found, restored, and rallied a half dozen Ferraris—and own more—and Jon takes those that are suited to it, such as his 250 GTO, vintage racing. He also has an extensive collection of Ferrari miniatures, and one of the biggest private collections of the marque's literature in the world.

There is the joy of owning and driving these cars, and also the thrill of the hunt. One of his prize possessions initially held the same honor for Italy's most famous film director.

If you've seen a car like this car before, you've seen this car. Built for Italian movie director, Roberto Rosselini, the silver coupe employs Ferrari 375 running gear and a special body crafted for Rosselini—at Ferrari's direction—by Sergio Scaglietti. The Shirleys acquired it in France from its owner of 25 years. *David Gooley*

Roberto Rosselini, lover of fast cars and beautiful women, had just married Ingrid Bergman, emerging cinema superstar. He wanted an extraordinary car, and was a man who could get Enzo Ferrari on the phone. The car Rosselini ordered in 1954 was originally a Ferrari 375 Pinin Farina Spider. It was a race car underneath, says Shirley—without even a cooling fan. The director had no quibbles with the car's performance, but he decided he wanted a coupe. He took it back to Ferrari, who sent it to Sergio Scaglietti, his race car builder, to fashion something appropriate.

The curvaceous silver coupe Scaglietti crafted served Rosselini well for 10 years, which Shirley could track through the little green tax book that accompanied the car. In 1964, Rosselini sold it to a man in Sicily, who let the taxes go. The car stopped running and was sitting in a warehouse in Palermo when a man from Paris bought it. He hauled it to France, put it in his underground garage, and partially disassembled it to begin a restoration. The beginning was all it saw. The car sat in pieces for a quarter century, during which the collector world lost track of it.

As it has from its early days, Ferrari remains committed to racing—pushing technology forward to give racers like Michael Schumacher what they need to win at the highest levels of the sport. A Formula 1 engine like this can wind out to revs approaching 20,000—higher than the average superbike. *David Gooley*

If this picture isn't making your mouth water, it's time to call your optometrist about a new prescription. What you're missing includes a Cobra, E-Type Jag, Porsche 550 Spider, Ferrari 250 GTO, 1956 T-Bird, Ferrari 275 GTS/4 NART (North American Racing Team) Spider (yellow car, center), Ford GT, and a Ferrari race transporter, among other gems. *David Gooley*

Rosselini's unique Ferrari 375 resurfaced in the early 1990s, when the Frenchman let it be known that the car was for sale. Various American dealers swooped in at the opportunity, yet the way they treated the seller put the man off. This was a very special car he had owned for 25 years and he wasn't just going to disgorge it for a fat check. He wanted an appropriate buyer.

A friend of Shirley's who knew of the car but hadn't gone after it mentioned it to Shirley and they agreed that it would be a fabulous car to restore and show. They needed a better angle than their competition, though. What they required was a contact who understood the seller's world.

Their efforts led them to an Englishman who had lived in France for many years and was married to a Frenchwoman. They engaged this man to help them convince the seller that their plans for the car would honor and preserve it. After several months, the seller was convinced. Jon and Mary flew to

The mezzanine upstairs, which includes the cases of Ferrari miniatures, overlooks the main collection on the floor below. The vented brake rotor on the coffee table has been turned into an ashtray—it would be a good idea to get permission before lighting up. *David Gooley*

France, where they, the seller, and his wife—along with their English friend and his wife—gathered in the owner's home. The owner had a pair of Bugattis in his garage too, which were also disassembled. The Shirleys came to understand that the seller's wife wanted him to restore one of the cars—presumably so they could use and enjoy it—and sell off the other two. Luckily, they had not chosen the Rosselini car to keep.

The parties drafted a brief contract in French and English. The seller got out some old photos of the Rosselini Ferrari and

finally he said, "Ça va." His wife opened a bottle of champagne, they toasted the deal, and the seller started to weep. The Shirleys smiled in sympathy—and said they'd wire the money immediately. Later, they had a second party in their hotel room with the couple that helped them land this extraordinary catch.

The car came to them in many boxes, which fortunately included small remnants of the seat material and headliner. Using the parts in hand, old photographs, and other details their research uncovered, the Shirleys restored the car to the original

The number 26 Ricci car, a Lampredi V-12-engined Ferrari 340/375 MM, was a works racer for the 1953 season. This car raced in top form at Spa and Le Mans, and also, as the paintwork indicates, in the Carrera Panamericana. *David Gooley*

specs as built by Scaglietti for Roberto Rosselini. Missing turn signals turned out to be stock Lancia items of the period—which they sourced—and they replaced absent headlights with correct Marchal items. It took from 1995 to the winter of 1997–1998 to finish the car and it has won numerous shows and awards since at venues such as Pebble Beach, Louis Vuitton, and Cavallino. The last show Mary handled on her own, as Jon was recovering from a knee injury from skiing. She took the car down to Florida, drove it to the Cavallino show, talked with the judges, and won Best in Show with it.

The Rosselini resides with the rest of the 30-car collection in a 15,000-square-foot space that also houses the miniatures. It includes a storage room and a space for mechanical work. The space is not open to the public, generally, but the Shirleys do make it available to various clubs and charities. The area Ferrari, Alfa Romeo, Fiat, and BMW clubs have all gathered there to meet and see the cars.

So far the Shirleys have restored six Ferraris—one on their own, and five professionally. Five have won first place at Pebble Beach and the one they restored themselves took third place, much to their satisfaction.

The gorgeous 1938 Alfa Romeo 2900 coupe was the supercar of its era, says Shirley, with many advanced features, including twin superchargers and all independent suspension. The long hood covers a straight-eight engine. Alfa produced about 40 of these cars and the location and history of virtually all of them are known. This is the only one whose louvers extend beyond the back of the hood line, which further accentuates the long front end. *David Gooley*

And what happens with the cars after they're shown? They get driven! Four of them have done the Mille Miglia, and Jon vintage races the ones appropriate for that level of competition. When the wear and tear of use takes them down to 70-point cars, they'll restore them again. And show them again. Then rally and race them again in the full spirit of the prancing horse.

The Ferrari legend remains strong in part because the cars live on, not just on quiet show stands—but snarling and clawing around racetracks and mountain switchbacks as they have done for generations. Not everyone hears the automobile's voice. The Shirleys do, and they strive to let it sing.

Ferrari is the garage's main focus and includes important examples. The number 20 car, a 1949 166MM, placed second in the Mille Miglia, won at Spa, and won the first race it entered in California in 1951. It rests beside stunning 1954 Ferrari 500 Mondial, California Spyder, and Daytona. At the end of the row are some non-Ferraris—an XK120 like Jon had before moving to California years ago, and an Austin Healey similar to one a friend of his had in their youth.
David Gooley

Gippo Salvetti

ALFA BLUE TEAM

Several interesting boats hang over the Alfa Romeo collection, including this small speed boat, which Salvetti saw abandoned in a field. He admired the styling, went to the owner, and bought it for $50 to restore and include with his car collection. Below it is a rare and beautifully styled 1967 Giulia Sprint Speciale, Salvetti's first car. *David Gooley*

In the 1970s, Gippo Salvetti's father was a captain of Italy's Squadra Azzura (Blue Team), which dominated competitors for many years. The contest was bridge, the strategic card game. Salvetti's father was a captain on the team that won the world championship three times. If bridge has been overshadowed by other pastimes in recent decades, in its day it was an intellectual challenge enjoyed by millions of people around the world. Being good at it was symbolic of a clever, agile mind, and brought the same sort of cachet James Bond earns in Ian Fleming's novel through his skill at baccarat.

Salvetti is proud of his father's accomplishments and those of Blue Team, whose name he has applied to his own passion: the Alfa Romeo. He has immersed himself in his version of the Squadra Azzura with the same zeal and passion as his father applied to world-championship cards.

Salvetti has one of the largest collections of postwar Alfa Romeos in the world. Apart from special cars outside of normal production (and including some of them, too), he has virtually every Alfa Romeo model made from 1947 through 1991,

The Alfa Blue Team collection includes this one-off Alfa Romeo 2500 Pininfarina built by the company for an important client for the Geneva car show in 1950. Salvetti bought the car in 1979. Beside it on the wall is a toy Giulietta Sprint spider made in 1960. Above that is a real car, though not the one it appears to be. It's a Giulia Super 1600 (not very valuable) restored as a Giulia TI Super Quadrifoglio race car (rare and expensive) clone. As Salvetti says, "it's very impressive for people to see a Giulia TI Super Quadrifoglio on the wall!" But it's a joke. *David Gooley*

Hard to believe this gas/electric range was produced shortly after World War II, when bomb damage left the Alfa Romeo factory unable to generate significant car production. They apparently had some ground to make up in price too, as Salvetti says the range cost as much as three cars of the period. He bought this one 25 years ago and it is one of very few remaining examples. He says, "It is a souvenir of Alfa Romeo objects that were built with a great deal of skill and refinement and precision." *David Gooley*

the cars whose designs he most appreciates. This covers 122 cars. He also owns eight Maseratis.

Alfa Blue Team functions as Salvetti's Alfa Romeo club. It occupies a 3,000-square-meter former foundry in Milan, Italy, and houses about 200 Alfa Romeos, including Salvetti's collection plus cars of other "team" members. Unlike his father's Blue Team, Salvetti's does not compete or race. His team is solely a club devoted to the Alfa Romeo marque and open only to Salvetti's friends. He started the club with four friends about 34 years ago when he bought the building. Its purpose is to celebrate the Alfa Romeo, to look at and talk about the cars, and to share stories about them. There are also repair facilities onsite and the club brings in a mechanic three times a week to help restore and maintain the club's holdings.

While the main focus of the club is Alfa Romeo, there are other dimensions to the collection. Central to their love of Alfa Romeos is an appreciation for mechanical and engineering genius. Salvetti and his fellow collectors do not like to see fine mechanical things abandoned or wasting away. As a result, Alfa Blue Team has gathered assortments of objects outside the automotive realm. These items include various

Gippo Salvetti started the Alfa Blue Team, an Alfa Romeo club, with four friends some 34 years ago, when he bought an old foundry and converted it to house his collection. Today it holds 200 cars, plus the club's collection of boats and movie cameras. *David Gooley*

Among the many more serious road cars is a little blue and yellow electric car (upper right) that Zagato used at Milanfiera—the Milan Car Exhibition during the 1970s and 1980s—to help people move among the car show grounds, which covered over two square kilometers. The car was good for about 10 miles per hour. Somewhat faster are Salvetti's red TZ1 and the Montreals flanking it in the adjacent corner. *David Gooley*

small boats—which hang on the facility's walls—as well as 200 to 300 movie (film) cameras.

The first Alfa Romeo Salvetti bought was a Giulia Sprint Speciale when he was 18 years old. He's been pursuing good examples of the marque ever since. In 2001, he started a publishing company called Fucina Editore in Milan. Fucina's books focus on cars and motorcycles, with an emphasis on personal experiences with the vehicles. Salvetti's own book, *Alfazioso*, was one of the company's early releases and tells, with flair and romance, many of the tales behind the cars he's collected over the decades.

His account of acquiring his Zagato 2600 SZ has an air of intrigue to it. Inspired by the few photos and reviews he'd seen, he had always wanted one but had never seen one in the

metal. When he did catch sight of the car, the timing was inopportune. He was enjoying a candlelit dinner and saw one pass by slowly on the street outside. He wanted to dash out the door and get a word with the owner before the chance was lost, but the woman accompanying him would not have understood. As consolation for his sudden shift in attention, he offered her a flower from a seller passing through the restaurant—an offer she declined. By the time they left the restaurant and he had the opportunity to make as inconspicuous a survey of the area as possible, the car was gone.

It may not be coincidence that he found himself in the same restaurant a few months later—this time with a group of people who wouldn't miss him for a moment if anything important appeared through the windows. It did—the same 2600 SZ he had seen before. Salvetti was out the door immediately. When he got outside, the car was parking and the same flower seller whose offerings his prior dinner companion refused stepped out. The man had acquired the car, by luck or by providence, in a game of cards. He collected his winnings but didn't feel quite at home in his rare sports car. He was happy to convert

An advantage to being both an Alfa owner and Gippo Salvetti's friend is that you can join Alfa Blue Team and take advantage of the club's work space and the mechanic they bring in three days a week to work on the club's cars. This 2600 Touring spider was built in 1964. Salvetti calls it rare but not extremely so and says it is capable of 120-plus miles per hour—pretty good for a car of this size and era. *David Gooley*

This 1985 Formula Boxer is a race car trainer designed to help young drivers learn how to race. Hanging on the wall above is a child's electric car with a style that fits in with the collection's other cars and boats. *David Gooley*

it to cash, and Salvetti was ready to make a deal—his reward for patience, persistence and a keen eye for his beloved manufacturer's striking designs, particularly those by Zagato.

Although his postwar Alfa Romeo collection is one of the most extensive in the world, Salvetti longs for one model that he does not yet own: the TZ2—sometimes referred to as "the Baby [Ferrari] GTO," according to *Sports Car Market*. He has a TZ1, the car's predecessor, but calls

the striking and agile TZ2 sports racer the most beautiful car ever made. Prices have surpassed the seven figure mark in U.S. dollars—more than Salvetti is willing to part with, even for such a magnificent car—but his eyes are open for the right opportunity and you can bet he'll be ready to strike if it arises.

Such is Salvetti's love of the Alfa Romeo that the Alfa Blue Team collection even bears a gas/electric range the company

Unique among the company's many sports car models is this jeep, the Matta, which in Italian means "crazy." It features the Alfa Romeo 1900's 1.9-liter engine and is one of only about 2,040 examples made. The Matta has a limited slip differential and is, according to Salvetti, a very good off-road vehicle. These cars are in a second floor room in the club's building. *David Gooley*

built immediately following the war, when bomb damage had left the company struggling to produce a product and stay in business. The range looks decades newer than its production date—a testament to the skill and style of Alfa Romeo's engineers and designers. Salvetti is not the only one who recognizes the piece's unique beauty and rarity. The only other one he knows of is in Alfa Romeo's Museum in Arese, near Milan.

In its early years, Alfa Romeo was one of the fastest and most impressive cars in the world, respected by the biggest manufacturers and the best drivers in racing. If its racing days receded as the decades passed, its dedication to style and sporting performance has never faded. It is a company capable of inspiring remarkable devotion, and Gippo Salvetti and Alfa Blue Team embody that love of the marque.

Another excellent watercraft in the collection is this wood motorboat made in 1960 by Cantieri Navali di Pisa, which also made big yachts. Salvetti restored this boat because of its beauty. *David Gooley*

Craig Ekberg

GEMS FROM THREE ERAS

Craig Ekberg's garage packs a lot of dream into a limited space. Another garage, below this one, holds a few more cars that are not quite this special. *Robert Genat*

For some car collectors, possession is enough. Other enthusiasts savor time at the wheel, while a third group likes to put their machines up against other fabulous vehicles in pursuit of best in class or best in show. Finally there are those whose obsession lies with the machinery itself, who turn wrenches to make the car function with a beauty equal to its lines. Craig Ekberg does it all.

The depth of his involvement accounts for his collection's comparatively limited scope. His main prizes are a brass era car, an early classic, and an iconic sporting machine from the 1950s. He knows them at the nut-and-bolt level. He could tear each one down to the last washer and rebuild it, which makes driving them that much more fun. If it runs like new, it's largely because he made it so.

With each acquisition, Ekberg reached further back in time. The first was his 300SL Gullwing, which he cherishes, drives, shows, and enters in historic races with himself at the wheel—naturally. From there he decided to get an "old car," a

Three pristine cars, three great eras. Much of the wall art has come from rallies and shows, but the red roadster, etched in glass, was made by an artist from a droptop 300SL that Ekberg had before the Gullwing. *Robert Genat*

Few examples of the legendary Stutz Bearcat remain for appreciative eyes, and fewer still for purchase. Ekberg discovered his 1915 Bearcat in his driveway when it was delivered there by a friend as a surprise. (Remind your own friends how high the bar has been set.) He and wife, Hanne, own Harleys, but they spend more time with the cars. *Robert Genat*

goal met by his 1931 Buick Sport Roadster. He hadn't planned to reach for an even earlier model, but a fellow collector, Jim Grundy, nudged him in that direction. Grundy had a brass-era car and, as enthusiasts often do, felt his friend Ekberg should too. When they would meet at shows, Grundy always asked, "Are you ready to buy one yet?" For a few years, the answer was no, but finally Ekberg became intrigued. Grundy said he'd start looking.

Perhaps a month later, Grundy called. "Will you be home this Saturday afternoon?" he asked.

"I could be," Ekberg replied. "Why?"

"Because your 'new' car will be delivered between 2 and 5."

"What is it?" Ekberg inquired.

"I'm not going to tell you," his friend said. "But if you don't want it, I'll take it."

That Saturday, Ekberg gathered his car-guy friends at his

The Ekbergs' cars see the show circuit and the vintage competition circuit. The couple enjoy touring too, and have made good friends in many countries who share their appreciation for the joy of motoring. *Robert Genat*

house, and they sat out by the driveway with champagne. The truck arrived, as Grundy had promised. What lay inside dispelled even the faintest reservations Ekberg might have had about buying a car older than his Buick. The brass-era treasure Grundy had found for him was a Stutz Bearcat, one of the defining automobiles of the period. Only one car, a Mercer Raceabout, could claim to be its equal. No, this one would not be going back to Grundy. It would not be leaving Ekberg's possession, ever.

Despite the car's rarity and age, Ekberg uses it as often as he can. He spent the better part of a year underneath it, making it drive just as it did when new. That's his passion—making his cars run the way they did when the manufacturer released them to the public. "Usually cars got famous because they were great cars, absolutely fabulous in their time," he explains. But over time, they get worked on, repaired, refurbished, ignored. They may continue to look good, but the refined performance fades. Ekberg brings it back. Carefully, meticulously. He drives it, listens to it, feels what it communicates to him through the controls, and makes a mental note. Then he tweaks, wrenches, zeroes in on and eliminates the shortcomings. "When you get these cars dialed in, they're awesome." He goes to equal lengths to make the car as original as possible, so that it's truly "as new" to the best of his ability.

Ekberg has always loved cars. His first sports car was a Porsche 914. He went through seven of them as a kid—buy one, fix it up, get it right, then do it again. He often sold cars he'd whipped into shape to meet other needs. Those days are behind

Making his cars run like the day they were built is a challenge this enthusiast cherishes as much as a spirited drive. And he does it with a devotion to complete originality. The Bearcat was nice when he got it, but he's been through it completely, himself, to make it run like the day it left the Stutz factory. *Robert Genat*

This low-mileage Merc doesn't just sit here looking good, or take light drives doing so. Ekberg vintage races this car, taking full advantage of its performance breeding and potential. *Robert Genat*

him, but he isn't a volume buyer—he only has what he can use. He and his wife, Hanne, make the most of their good fortune, doing tours, car shows, charity events, and historic races. They love the camaraderie of the car culture, which has brought them friends all over the world. "I couldn't do all of these things without a wife who enjoys it as much as I do," he says.

The garage is actually bigger than it appears, with three stalls above ground and three below. His cherished

three cars sit above. Ekberg had plans to build a bigger garage—he still entertains the notion—but this one cleaned up well. He painted it, laid a linoleum floor, and found wall space for all of the posters, trophies, ribbons, and memorabilia they've collected over the years of driving, showing, and racing the cars. They only collect memorabilia as it collects on its own, with just a few pieces bought as car art for art's sake. Ekberg concedes that a crunch lies ahead, though, as

When they bought this 1931 Buick Sport Roadster, the Ekbergs considered it their "old car." Fellow collector Jim Grundy worked on Ekberg for years to get him to reach back further, for a machine from the brass era. *Robert Genat*

Not everything he drives is decades old. His daily driver today is a Toyota pickup. He's had a string of new Ferraris too, searching perhaps for a day-to-day experience on par with the feeling he gets at the wheel of the Stutz or the Gullwing. For the most part, it isn't there. Sure, his F-40 was a fun car, and he used it to its full potential, but newer vehicles he still finds lacking. For this fundamentally hands-on guy, new cars intrude too much on the driver's domain, insulating him from the sensations and the forces a true driver needs to feel and control.

In the old days, he notes, a good driver could win in a bad car. That's the period that appeals to Ekberg, when man and machine pushed speed's boundaries in synchronicity. It's why he loves vintage racing. The 300SL Gullwing was an undiluted car, rewarding if you held your foot down through the turn—punishing otherwise. He's had his Bearcat in a four-wheel drift. This is what great machines were designed to do. This is what Ekberg tunes them to do again.

The thrill of on-the-edge driving may have inspired him to take up flying, where you can soar in three dimensions. Like his cars, his war bird, a Chinese Nanchang CJ6, is in flawless condition—a show winner like the cars, and used just as thoroughly. Since he bought it, he and his wife have added air shows to their calendar, and Ekberg has learned to fly in formation, a unique challenge for pilot and plane.

But the aircraft won't displace the cars. Both are dear to the Ekbergs. "Every time a car guy goes to an event or auction, he thinks he should have whatever he sees. I like all cars, and that's the problem. But there's no end to the sickness." He'll stay with what he can use.

"I'm very lucky to have the cars that I have," he says. "When I open the garage door and look at my cars, it's really exciting."

the walls have absorbed about all they can, and he and Hanne have no plans to stop enjoying the events from which the decorations come.

His approach to repairs is comparable to that of other collectors with fine garages. What's simple gets done here. More invasive operations go down at either of two nearby shops, whose owners are Ekberg's friends—typically with Ekberg manning the tools.

Absent blistering performance, antique cars derive a lot of their appeal from craftsmanship and attention to detail—though Ekberg also loves the way old cars feel on the road. *Robert Genat*

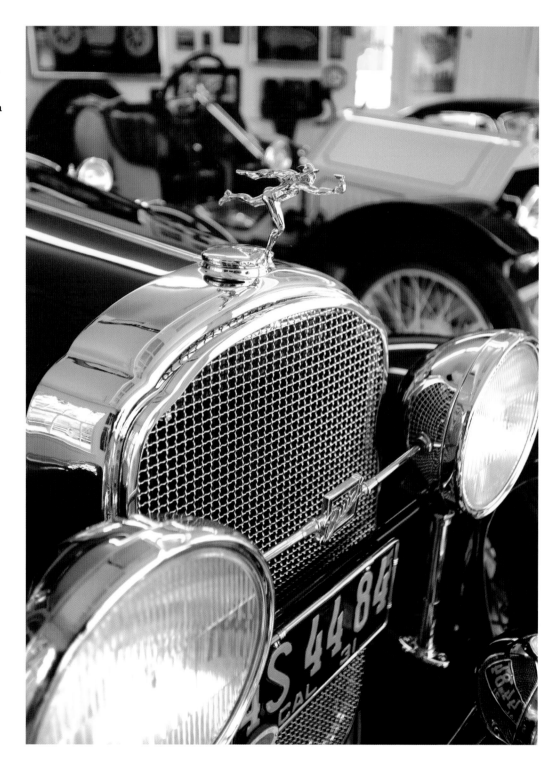

THE JOY OF COLLECTING

"I've always loved to collect things. I can't tell you why."

— *collector extraordinaire, Ron Nardone*

Stephen Johns

"ALL THESE LOVELY THINGS"

The Bentley Speed Six is not a go-kart but a pedal car, one of three in the collection. Not shown are another Bentley and an Austin. "They're beautifully made," says Stephen Johns, and fairly modern. They go for nearly as much as an old car, but he likes their reduced space requirements. *James Mann*

Stephen Johns had a big textile mill in Yorkshire that gave him the means to collect cars and many other objects, but not the time to enjoy them fully, or to let others do so. Once he retired, he concluded: "I have all these lovely things, and I should let people look at them." Retirement brought Stephen to Exmoor, a coastal region of Somerset, much of which is protected as national park, National Trust property, nature reserves, and Heritage coast. Here, he put his collection of cars, motorcycles, and memorabilia on public display in a museum open to the public every Thursday, or any time by appointment.

Initially, the museum was open four days a week, but Stephen found that keeping up that pace didn't allow him to enjoy the collection as much as he wanted to, or to pursue other pastimes. The one-day and by-appointment schedule strikes a happy balance, giving the public a fixed opportunity they can count on, but also permitting the many clubs who enjoy making the trip to this vacation area to get in on their own for a private visit.

Less time hosting visitors also allows Stephen more opportunity to drive his cars. They all run, and he gets them out onto the roads to keep everything working properly. "I don't like museum pieces," he says, which may be why the word "museum" does not appear in the name of his operation. He calls it "The Exmoor Classic Car Collection," though its pieces range far

A mezzanine above the main floor holds BSA Bantams, which the post office used for telegram deliveries in the 1960s and 1970s. Johns Stephen has a lot of post office memorabilia, including uniforms, satchels, and even old telegrams. *James Mann*

Britain's Automobile Association has supported drivers since 1905. These two modified motorcycles take a different approach to the utility vehicle, the BSA offering cargo space behind the driver, while the Dot has its two wheels and box up front. Along the wall is a Le Mans miniature collection featuring every winner of the last century, with corresponding national flags. *James Mann*

beyond the typical four-wheeled conveyance. "I like groups of things," he says. Once he takes to a particular creation, be it a motorcycle, helmet, model, grease gun, or foot pump, to name a few, others will likely join it.

"I started with cars in the 1960s," Stephen recalls. He's been adding to the collection ever since, whenever something strikes his fancy. Just what that might be is hard to predict, though everything that comes in is appealing to look at—from his Speed Six Bentley pedal car to his (full size) 1933 Austin butcher's truck.

He recently bid on a 1930s Rolls-Royce 20/25 that Harrods had used as a courtesy car for its customers. It was painted Harrods' green and black and included the uniform worn by the chauffeur, who assisted customers to their homes after a day of shopping. The bidding came down to Stephen and one other man, but he could sense his rival was determined to get it. Stephen let it go when the price topped what he felt the car was worth.

The Harrods car would have tied in nicely with the collection, as Stephen already has two distinctive Rolls-Royces, as well as

Stephen gets his vehicles onto the roads regularly to keep them in good working order. He always gets a big smile from Exmoor inhabitants when he cruises the roads in his old London taxi. The background here suggests the breadth of the collection, which includes clarinets, coffee mugs, and cricket gear. *James Mann*

service vehicles that were operated by uniformed drivers. He collects uniforms too. The old London taxi includes an appropriately attired mannequin driver—occasionally replaced by Stephen on the streets around the village. "Faces light up when you come along," he says. He also has vehicles and uniforms related to the GPO, the old General Post Office, and the AA, Britain's roadside recovery service.

The post office vehicles are a set of three BSA Bantam motorcycles, which the GPO used for telegram delivery in the 1960s and 1970s. The AA also used BSAs, as well as bikes from other English manufacturers. One of the more unique bikes in the collection is a Dot ("Devoid of Trouble") brand motorcycle with a front cargo box—a bit like the pedal contraptions vendors sometimes use for selling ice cream in the summer, though with motorized power. During wartime, these three-wheelers were used to deliver bombs, Stephen says—not a cargo he would want to carry in a nose-heavy motor trike that has awkward

This 1933 Austin truck was used for butcher shop deliveries. It drives well, but it's quite small. "You couldn't get a set of golf clubs in the back," notes Stephen. *James Mann*

Among the car memorabilia is this collection of vintage spark plugs, which shows a great range of sizes in the holes they fit in and the wrenches required to remove them. *James Mann*

Model cars offer the most variety for the space required. The Exmoor Classic Car Collection features hundreds of models, including a large assortment of buses and work trucks. *James Mann*

This Bridgestone 100 TMX motorcycle is a rare, though capable, bike produced in Japan by the tire company of the same name. Behind it is an extensive collection of model cars. *James Mann*

handling even when it's empty. Dot was one of numerous small manufacturers who bought engines from someone else, here Villiers, and built their own designs around them.

Another three-wheeled creation in the collection is a 1933 Morgan, which was new when Stephen was born. "It goes like a bomb," he says, "but it's a bugger to drive." The front engine—extremely front—runs through a two-speed crash box (no synchros), which Stephen says is "nearly an impossible box." Fortunately, he can usually pull away in second without downshifting. This is important, given the other challenges the car presents: The front two wheels use a hand brake, while the rear

uses a brake pedal, and the throttle is by hand. "You need three hands to drive it," Stephen laughs. "When you think that drivers used to round Brooklands at over 100 miles per hour in these things—they must have been crazy."

The French had it right several years earlier, with the 1927 Type 40 Bugatti. "This is one of the nicest cars to drive in the collection," Stephen notes. "It makes a lovely noise." The Bugatti has a crash box too. "You've got to keep the revs up," he advises, "and change down at high revs. When you get it right, it goes in like butter."

Shifting is most curious in his 1938 D70 Delage, which uses a Cotal electromagnetic gearbox. You start off with a

Two of Stephen's collection favorites, a 1927 Bugatti Type 40 and 1938 D70 Delage. While some machines in the collection are tricky to drive, these perform wonderfully if driven with care and a little experience. *James Mann*

clutch, then once under way, move a knob on the steering column. From that point, the gearbox does the shifting on its own with no more clutching. "It will keep up with modern traffic," says Stephen, and was "such a super car to drive in its day. It left most contemporaries behind." The only drawback to the Delage is the gearbox's complexity. "How on earth did somebody start

from scratch and design a gearbox like that?" he wonders. Luckily, he has found repair diagrams in English, though he wouldn't tackle work of that sort on his own.

Stephen does some things on the cars, but mostly basic things. He was too busy working in the textile business during the years when most people hone their mechanical skills, and there was no

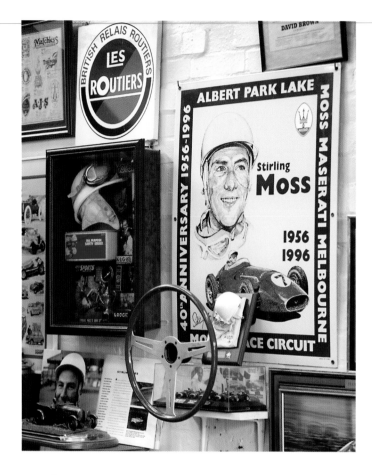

The collection includes a lot of memorabilia relating to Stirling Moss and his career, including a signed steering wheel. As Stephen puts it, "I've always had a lot of room for Stirling." *James Mann*

pressure to do so because he had people around who could handle it. He takes on some straightforward repairs, even replacing the head gasket on his MG PA. But he also has friends who are skilled engineers and who don't mind troubleshooting Stephen's intriguing classics—especially since the work gets tested on Exmoor's scenic roads afterward. Stephen also enjoys keeping the cars clean and polished.

The garage the collections occupy is an old post office maintenance building, where vehicles were washed and repaired. What Stephen liked about it when he saw it was a long wall, about 35 feet, big enough to hold his collection of Le Mans models and posters. The garage is located in Minehead, an Exmoor town so old it is said to be mentioned in the Domesday Book from 1086. What's surprising is that the name has nothing to do with mines or mining. Instead it comes from the Celtic word for mountain.

"The highest point in Somerset is just in front of our house," Stephen says. "Absolutely gorgeous." The area also suits his other hobbies, like gardening, cooking, and playing golf. In this coastal region, he plays on a links course—the seaside version of the game laid out along the natural terrain—which can be challenging, but Stephen has some experience. During the season, he's played a round at least once a week for 64 years, since age 9.

Retirement here, in a coastal town, with his collections, hobbies, and wonderful surroundings is treating Stephen and his wife well. "My golfing buddy and I bore ourselves to death talking about how wonderful it is here, and how lucky we are," he laughs. "But it's true."

With its spoke wheels, V-twin engine, and long side exhaust pipe, the Morgan looks as much vintage motorcycle as car. Beside it is a piece of British motorcycle history, one of the last Triumph Bonnevilles to come from the original factory, before the company's rebirth. *James Mann*

Below the helmet collection hang a few more pieces related to the post office: drawings of ornate interiors going back to the 1920s and 1930s. *James Mann*

Stephen was too busy running a business to become an expert mechanic, but he does what he can. He pulled the cylinder head on this MG PA to replace the head gasket, for example. The Rolls is a 20-horsepower model from 1927. Neckties overhead are all from oil companies and were given to Stephen by a friend who drove a tanker truck to supply filling stations. *James Mann*

Dave & Ron Simon

"NOW APPEARING IN ..."

Cars, movies and airplanes are among the main themes for the Cornwell and Sheridan collection, owned by Dave and Ron Simon. The vehicles have been purchased over the years, but much of the memorabilia—like the Texaco sign—is donated by friends and visitors who have the items but lack room to display them. *David Gooley*

The party-crasher is part real, part painting. The nose, engine, and bent prop are real Stearman biplane items. The bricks are both painted images and three-dimensional items hung from wire. *David Gooley*

What do the movies *Ed Wood, Chinatown, The Aviator, The Great Race,* and *Gone in 60 Seconds*—the original and the remake—have in common? The same thing the famous Grey Poupon commercial with the two Rolls-Royces has in common with several TV spots for Victoria's Secret lingerie. All feature cars from Dave and Ron Simon's collection in Southern California. In addition to cars, their garage holds motorcycles, airplanes, signs from gas

One of only two cars without its original factory engine is this blue hot rod, like one Dave bought at age 14. There's a Merc flathead under the hood. The paint once had flames and other youthful touches but Dave prefers it more subtle today. The motorcycle on the wall is an "unauthorized" factory-style Yamaha road racing bike that Ron and his partner built and campaigned in the late 1960s and early 1970s. *David Gooley*

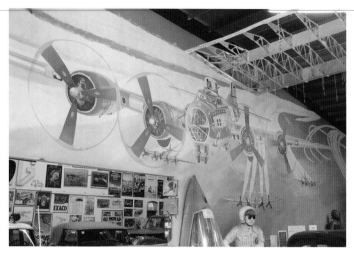

Dave Simon and a fellow pilot cobbled this Aircoupe (or Ercoupe) together from various pieces sourced at an aircraft junkyard. It's too big to come into the garage in one piece, so it was assembled beneath this spot, painted in military colors, and raised. *David Gooley*

This mural covers a wall 75 feet long and 14 feet high and shows B-17 bombers and German Messerschmitts engaged in aerial combat during World War II. The "skeleton plane," whose wing is visible in the upper corner, is a Stinson 108 Voyager from about 1938 to 1940. *David Gooley*

stations and auto parts manufacturers, and a range of aviation items, such as instruments from World War II aircraft, both Allied and Axis powers.

They call their vehicle assortment the Cornwell and Sheridan Collection. The name gives it a British feel, which is appropriate since the brothers used to race MG TCs in their youth, and Dave started out collecting British cars. There's more to the name, though, and some visitors pause, stare at the company logo and ask why it sounds so familiar. Invariably those people have some connection to the Boyle Heights section of East Los Angeles. That's where two streets, Cornwell and Sheridan, intersect. The Simons grew up near that intersection.

The facility used to hold inventory for their appliance parts business—at least that was the justification for building it. The real reason, Dave admits, was to house the cars. They started collecting around 1960. Dave bought a Model A Ford and restored it, then did the same with two more. He enjoyed it, but by the third Ford, he realized he could restore some higher end cars without expending much more money or effort. He

branched out to Buicks, Cadillacs, Rolls-Royces, and other cars that had style he admired.

Dave was in outside sales for their appliance business. He traveled extensively around Southern California supplying the shops that would send repairmen out to fix refrigerators, dishwashers, ovens. He always made these journeys in a collector car, mainly because he enjoys them but it also made him the easiest salesman to identify.

"'You know, the guy with the old cars.'

'Oh, Dave Simon, sure, I know him. . . .'"

Though he's retired, he still drives classics, picking out a different one every three days. "It's like a Chinese fire drill," says Dave. "To get one car out, I have to move a half-dozen." But it keeps all of the cars in operating condition and ensures that each sees regular maintenance. It's fun, and he gets a lot of attention from other motorists and pedestrians wherever he drives or parks.

The downside is that they do break down. "Those are always embarrassing situations," says Dave. "You're in terrible

The Army items have found their way into the collection from Dave's love of aviation, including military planes. The weapon on the tripod is a genuine World War II–era .30-caliber machine gun. The fiberglass soldier came out of another car collection in Gardenia, California, which didn't fit as well there because that collection had no military theme. The Simons acquired the fireman model behind the MG TC (photo, p. 173) from the same collector. *David Gooley*

If this submarine looks a little too strange to be real, it is. The two-ton prop is from the 1965 film, *The Great Race*, and is one of three vehicles from the film owned by Cornwell and Sheridan. The bike in front is not from the film; it's a 1940 BSA military model. *David Gooley*

traffic and all of a sudden the battery dies"—which recently happened. Another time, he was in a 1949 Rolls-Royce Silver Wraith and the fuel pump quit. The car died in bumper-to-bumper traffic. Yet here's where driving a beautiful vintage automobile has its advantages. He climbed out to push the car to the side of the road and all of sudden people came from all directions. People were hopping out of their cars to help him get this gorgeous Roller out of harm's way.

Over the years, the collection has taken on a life of its own and become a gathering point for enthusiasts of all ages. The Simons call it "the Boys Club." It isn't all boys, though. Visitors of all sorts use and enjoy the space. The main room holds the Simons collection of about 49 vehicles. A second room, roped off, contains cars other collectors pay to store there. They all love the atmosphere, which is more a social club than a storage facility. Collectors stop over to visit, work on their cars, trade stories, and have lunch.

Dave has eight grandchildren and loves kids. He opens the collection to Boy Scouts, Girl Scouts, car clubs, fund raisers, and other groups and events. "When kids come here, we have the cars open. They can get in them, sit in the driver's seat of a Rolls-Royce. They really enjoy it. There's always something going on here," he says, "at least every other weekend. We also have regular 'car nights,' with a live band, hot dogs, chili. . . . It's grown on its own."

Keeping 49 antique and classic vehicles on the road requires a well stocked shop. Dave Simon does nearly all the work himself and has most every tool, lubricant, cleaner, washer, nut, and bolt on hand to finish the job. If less attractive than the cars and memorabilia, it's just as important to the garage. *David Gooley*

The main storage and display space lies behind an anteroom with access to the roads beyond. Dave likes to drive a different car from the collection every three days, which requires some regular juggling and forces him to keep all the cars in running order—even though he would anyway. *David Gooley*

The collection derives from various sources and interests. Dave is a pilot and has another good friend who also flies and who used to restore Stearman biplanes. He had a supply of old engines, propellers, instruments, and various other extra parts. As a display for the garage, they took an engine and prop, attached it to the front half of a fuselage and painted it to look like a plane crashing through the brick wall. They also mocked up another civilian plane to look like an army bomber—they bought it piece-meal at an airplane junkyard and assembled it inside the garage. They raised the "bomber" with forklifts and bolted it to the ceiling.

The movie angle, like the car gatherings, has also developed its own momentum. Rent a few cars to Hollywood and if everybody's happy with the deal, more inquiries come. The collection includes vehicles they've rented to the studios, and also a few curiosities that got screen time before the Simons acquired them. They own three creations from Blake

Ron Simon had British cars in his early days, and both brothers own MG TCs, which they raced in the late 1950s and early 1960s. The Mobil Pegasus is among the large items this warehouse, with its 14-feet-tall walls, is capable of displaying. War planes fit in with the collection's aviation theme. *David Gooley*

Edwards' whacky car film, *The Great Race*, with Jack Lemmon and Tony Curtis. Cornwell and Sheridan have the submarine, the *Hannibal 8*—which raises up and down—and Professor Fate's torpedo. Only the submarine remains on site. The *Hannibal 8* and torpedo are on loan to the Peterson Museum.

If the planes on display have been cobbled together for fun, this is not the case with the cars. Though he restored a few in his youth, Dave seeks original, unrestored cars for the collection. Only two of the 49 do not have their original engine. One is a hot rod like one he bought when he was 14 years old. It has a 1953 Merc flathead—wrong for the car but plenty right for a hot rod. The other is one of the Lincoln Continentals, which has a 390 Ford engine. Everything else in the collection is virtually 100 percent stock.

In addition to driving the cars, Dave also does all the maintenance and any restoration work, except for painting

A variety of art and artifacts, including a Willys-Overland Jeepster grille circa 1948, cover the walls throughout the garage and shop. *David Gooley*

This is Dave's MG TC, which he took on his honeymoon. The bigger cars in his collection have made this one seem small by comparison. Though he still enjoys it, the TC would not be his first choice from the collection for a long tour today. *David Gooley*

This 1940 Plymouth convertible has appeared with Jack Nicholson and Johnny Depp in *Chinatown* and *Ed Wood*, respectively. Simon says his key to renting cars to Hollywood is to stay with it throughout the shoot. That way everyone knows how it was used and there are no arguments over scratches, etc. *David Gooley*

(which he stopped doing about 10 years ago) and upholstery. He works on the engines, does brakes, rear ends, and transmissions. Working on the cars and keeping them in good shape for his own use and Hollywood's is part of the collection's appeal for the Simons. There's always something to do, and usually someone to talk to.

All things considered, it's a nice retirement—driving and maintaining an assortment of beautiful cars, and sharing them with friends, youngsters, car clubs, charities, and studios. It's a good life for the cars too—to be used, cherished, looked after, and shared with a broad and appreciative audience.

Mario Righini

A CAR'S HOME IS ITS CASTLE

The main Righini collection resides in his fifteenth-century castle, which was operated as a winery before he bought it. Today it houses one of the largest private car collections in Italy, with many important cars, plus tractors, motorcycles, and carriages. *David Gooley*

The earliest cars in the collection date to the early 1900s and before—still youthful compared to their castle home. Among the oldest cars are a Benz and De Dion from the nineteenth century. There are also many early twentieth-century vehicles, like this 1920s Lancia Lambda. *David Gooley*

Automobile collectors will travel long distances in search of special cars. How much easier it would be if their owners dropped them off. For hundreds of worthy machines, and a few extraordinary ones, this has been Mario Righini's good fortune. His father started the family salvage business before World War II—and the vehicles poured in. The business recycled most of them, yet if a car was whole and in good shape, his father did not break it up. He was not a collector by nature, but by default. What came in and was not destroyed formed part of a huge collection of cars, boats, planes, motorcycles, tractors, scooters, and other machinery.

Righini's collection is so large it is stored in several places. Some things, such as the planes and boats, are too big to house indoors. They still occupy the grounds of the salvage business in the Emilia-Romagna countryside. But the best things, his favorites, fill a nearby castle built in the fifteenth century. He bought it from a family that once made wine, and converted it into a sort of medieval showroom for his classic and antique vehicles. It contains about 100 rooms, including the small ones, and houses many of his 300 cars. About 100 of them are Alfa Romeos. There are also motorcycles, tractors, and carriages. The third location was built in the eleventh or twelfth century on top of Roman ruins. He stores some vehicles in the space above, and has cheese and wine in the lower, Roman portion.

Cars and motorsports have been in Righini's blood since childhood, when he used to sit at the roadside and watch the Mille Miglia. He did this every year until the terrible crash of 1957

Peeking out from behind this door is an important vehicle from a legendary builder. It is one of the first two cars Enzo Ferrari built after leaving Alfa Romeo: the 815 Auto Avio Costruzioni. Ferrari built two, but only this one survives. *David Gooley*

Mario Righini collects cars and other vehicles for pleasure, but also to preserve them for posterity. He regularly opens his doors to the public. Righini's father started a scrap yard, and Mario joined the family business. The collection began from Righini Sr.'s reluctance to tear apart cars and other vehicles that were interesting and complete. *David Gooley*

brought an end to the event that spurred the Italian performance car industry and launched many racing stars. Righini's father even drove in the race, twice—in 1947 and 1948—with a Lancia Aprilia. He was not set on winning, however. To recruit participants, Pirelli offered them free tires, a valuable commodity just after the war. As Righini describes his father's campaign, "Papa set off with his four brand-new tires, but retired after 5 or 10 kilometers, claiming to have been beset by bad luck." The good luck was that he had four new tires, whose useful life he was looking to spread further than one grueling, thousand-mile race.

The Righini collection contains several race cars. Among them is an Alfa 2300 Monza, one of his favorites. "It is undoubtedly the finest racing car of its era," he says. It's also the car in which racing legend Tazio Nuvolari won the Italian championship. Righini has the car of another champion Italian racer, too—Alberto Ascari, Ferrari's first great driver. This machine, the 815 Auto Avio Costruzioni, is one of the first two cars Enzo Ferrari built after leaving Alfa Romeo. Ascari raced this 815 in the 1940 Mille Miglia, and the car bears his signature on the valve cover. Righini has competed many times in the revival Mille Miglia in another of his favorite cars, an Alfa 1750.

Along with cars, Righini also collects motorcycles and once embarked on a racing career. He campaigned a Morini— manufactured not far from his home—but a bad crash convinced him that his time was better spent off the racetrack. *David Gooley*

Righini's first car was a secondhand Alfa Romeo 1900, which he followed with a new Giulietta. In the 1950s, he started collecting cars on his own, purposefully, along with the cars his father set aside. He wanted to own nice cars for pleasure and also to conserve them for the future. Many of the cars both he and his father gathered were Alfa Romeos, their favorite marque. The collection even includes an early Romeo tractor, which Nicola Romeo built before buying Alfa and becoming an auto manufacturer. It is one of about 50 antique tractors that reside among the rest of the sprawling and varied collection.

Also among the Alfas are cars that Benito Mussolini owned and was photographed with many times. They were part of Mussolini's government fleet. Righini also owns an Alfa Romeo police car from the 1940s, when public unrest was high. The car is bulletproof but with an open top, allowing police to stand up and fire on the unruly. Righini remembers police doing so in Milan and Rome. He will save a vehicle with an important past even if that history was troubling. Future generations can benefit either way. There are warbirds among his planes, and he has two tanks, a personnel carrier, and various Jeeps abandoned by the Americans after the war.

He even has a car connected to the Pope—a Chrysler Imperial. He bought it from one of the Vatican mechanics. When American priests came to Rome, they sometimes brought their cars, which were too big for Italy's ancient streets. A scooter is more realistic transportation and these vehicles are everywhere in Italy's big cities. Many scooters found their way to the salvage yard and those too good to break up have become part of the Righini collection.

Righini's hundreds of vehicles cannot be contained even in the castle-garage that houses the main collection. These scooters and coupes, saved from the cutting torch, exist outside under modest shelter. Righini also has a large assortment of old and rare parts, and he collaborates with the Alfa Romeo museum to provide parts for significant models in their holdings. *David Gooley*

Set as it is in the countryside, the Righini salvage yard was the last resting place for area tractors. As with the cars, the family preserved many of these that were complete. Steel-wheeled machines are early examples. The collection includes a Romeo tractor, built by Nicola Romeo, the man who later created Alfa Romeo. *David Gooley*

The Alfa Romeo 2300 Monza driven by Tazio Nuvolari is a star in the collection. Righini calls it, "undoubtedly, the finest race car of its era." He says, "The integrity of the early Alfa mechanicals is high. The gearbox is a joy to use—precise and light—and it is sweet to drive, with decent roadholding." The cars share space with the motorcycle collection, which wraps around the main hall behind them. *David Gooley*

Among the older competition cars is this Amilcar from the mid- to late-1920s. The French Amilcar was light and nimble and very successful in hillclimbs. *David Gooley*

Most of the cars in the collection predate 1960, but this curvaceous Alfa Romeo TZ-1 gives up nothing in style to the older cars. Behind it is an Alfa 1900 from the 1950s. *David Gooley*

Motorcycles are also popular in Italy and Righini has a large assortment in the castle. His bikes by Morini, Ducati, MM, and CM were built nearby. He even bought a Morini to race, but he quit that pursuit after a serious accident. The motorcycle collection includes many fine and rare models, such as the Gilera Saturno Sport and a 1940 Bianchi Corsa with a supercharged 500-cc four-cylinder engine.

The oldest vehicles assembled under the castle-garage's vaulted ceilings are nineteenth-century carriages—they seem quite at home in their surroundings. They're here mainly for their beauty and history, but they also provide a convenient means for visitors to

This Cisitalia D46 Monoposto was one of Italy's first successful postwar racing cars, utilizing a then-advanced tubular chassis. This example was raced by legendary driver, Tazio Nuvolari. *David Gooley*

The collection's historically significant vehicles include this former government car from the Mussolini era. Military history is one of Mario Righini's passions and his sprawling collection includes a number of air, land, and sea vehicles related to the war. *David Gooley*

compare firsthand the early wheeled conveyances against the later horseless examples. Many of the carriages are from the 1860s to 1880s. Also among them is the inside of a campanile clock tower. The campanile, a freestanding bell tower, is one of the structures Italy is known for, particularly the Leaning Tower of Pisa. Righini was fortunate enough to preserve the works of one of them for the collection and posterity.

He owns one of the largest vehicle collections in Europe, but Righini does not have every car he admires. "I really want a Duesenberg," he says. "When I was visiting the United States, I saw the collection in Las Vegas, and I grew a passion for Duesenbergs. Maybe a Cord, too. Also a Maybach—those were beautiful cars." Not too many people are scrapping Cords and Duesenbergs these days, yet the collection reaches well beyond "found" items. Righini has cars by Ferrari, Maserati, and Lamborghini, a Mercedes 300SL Gullwing, and prewar BMW 328. Some of his vehicles are unique, like the Farina-bodied Fiat 8V that Roberto Rosselini gave to Ingrid Bergman, and Mussolini's Alfa Romeo Berlina.

With its vast collection gathered like horses in an ancient stable, Righini's castle makes for a peaceful setting in which to view so much mechanical history. He often opens the doors to groups of schoolchildren so they can see what their forebears produced for pleasure, travel, tilling, and racing. Many of the vehicles are unrestored, showing their age and experiences. This fits Righini's view of them as historically significant objects. "If the cars are in decent condition," he says, "there is no need to restore it, just conserve it."

Alfa Giulietta SZ-2 rests opposite a yellow Ferrari. Cars by Lotus and Lancia round out this room's exotics. *David Gooley*

Ron Nardone

FILL'ER UP

Lots of people come to Nardo's gate to peer in at the amazing garages and related road art. Often, he invites them in. Street rodders come here even when the gate is closed to photograph their cars by the gas pumps on either side. These pumps were used in the 1940s and 1950s, Nardo says, and fit well here because they're relatively short. *David Gooley*

Ron Nardone collects many things related to cars and car culture. A newer phase of the collection is his Tonka trucks, which he got into about five years ago. This is a small sample of that collection. He's currently building a reproduction of an old general store to house them. The trophies are mementos he's won with his 1938 Chevy school bus. *David Gooley*

When he was just a kid in the 1950s, Ron Nardone started to collect things such as old signs. His father said, "You can keep that stuff, but you have to put it in the garage. I don't want to see it from the street." Today, people love to see what he's gathered over the years. Their interest makes his assortment of gas station signs, pumps, and other memorabilia worth it. People stop over with their street rods to photograph them by the old Shell pumps at his gate. Others drive up just to gawk at the three full-size reproduction service stations he's built on the property, each bearing its own collectibles. If he's around, he'll usually open the gate and invite them in for a closer look.

He's always loved to collect things. "I can't tell you why," he says. But a lot of people are glad he does. Little, if any, of what he owns is still made in that form or style, and much of this memorabilia exists only in the hands of collectors and museums. With a few exceptions—the ones Nardone and his peers hope to find—the rest of these historical pieces have been scrapped, or have deteriorated to the point of no return.

Here is the big Richfield sign, porcelain and neon and 14 feet high. This eagle spread its wings above a small Nevada town for decades. The sign was made in 1937, though the previous owner told Nardone his family put it up in 1941. Lots of people stopped to share stories about the sign as Nardo took it down, but none offered to buy it. That's probably for the best, as no one else was likely to display it in the way the company originally intended, as it is here. *David Gooley*

Nardone found this 1935 Chevy front end with running boards at a swap meet. Nobody was interested in it until Nardo bought it, then everyone wanted it. On a whim, he decided to see if it would fit around this cedar tree and it did, perfectly. He is repairing the headlights and wiring them to shine out over the property at night. *David Gooley*

Shell items form a large portion of Nardo's collection. In addition to signs, gas pumps, and oil cans, he has many smaller mementos the stations used to hand out to customers, including tie clips, coat brushes, fishing lures, nail clippers, lighters, rulers, golf balls, and hangers to hold your jacket in the back of the car. *David Gooley*

This 1947 Crosley pickup is a rare vehicle, which used to belong to one of Nardo's friends. The paint is Nardo's own design, reflecting his mocked-up Shell station. At 6 feet 6inches, Nardo doesn't drive the Crosley much. He tends to take the 1938 Chevy school bus that sits behind it—it fits him much better. He often picks up friends in the bus and they take a drive and stop for dinner. Everybody likes the old school bus and with a 502 V-8 under the hood, it never holds up traffic. *David Gooley*

At 3,500 to 4,000 square feet, this garage is the largest of Nardo's reproduction service stations. His three favorite stations are Shell, Richfield, and Signal. The right-side wall here is done up like a Signal station. *David Gooley*

Nardone began collecting gas station memorabilia in the mid-1960s, before it became popular. Every time a gas station remodeled, it got rid of its old signs and pumps. More often than not, the station owner considered the old stuff junk and was content to be rid of it. And Nardone was happy to oblige. Even when an old station had nothing to offer, he photographed it to preserve the image. By the late 1970s, his collections had grown large enough that he needed more space to house them. What did he build for that purpose? Service stations, of course.

Using his many photographs for inspiration, Nardone has constructed three full-size reproduction service stations on his seven-and-a-half acre property. Together they hold a vast assortment of oil cans, product and service signs, Tonka trucks, gas pumps, and related memorabilia. He inventoried everything

in recent years but the collection moves on. He travels a lot and hits every swap meet in his area.

For some of the things he collects, such as large signs, he doesn't have much competition. Few other people have the room to store or display them. But unwieldy size makes these items rare for the same reason—what can't be easily moved or stowed is usually scrapped. His biggest sign, and one of his favorites, is a Richfield service station sign made in 1937. Featuring a bald eagle in flight, the sign is 14 feet high and over 9 feet wide.

A friend of Nardone's spotted the sign on a closed Richfield station in the center of a small town in Nevada. Nardone tracked down the owner—the grandson of the woman whose family once ran the station—and offered to buy it. The

Ron Nardone has collected things since childhood, with "road art" among his favorite genres. In his youth, his father tolerated the collection but wanted his signs stowed in the garage, where they couldn't be seen from the street. Today, people go out of their way to see all the things once familiar on America's roadways that have now disappeared or changed beyond recognition from their original forms. Around the shows and swap meets, he's known as "Nardo." *David Gooley*

This sign is a reproduction. The attendant in this paint scheme wears Coca-Cola insignias, though he's based on an original sign from Texaco. Coke "button" signs were among the earliest things Nardo collected in his youth and he still has a lot of "pop" collectibles. The Veltex sign came from a collector in Oregon, while the Wood River one behind it was found in a small Nebraska town. *David Gooley*

man agreed, but he made a suggestion. People in town liked the sign, he said; so if anyone asked what was going on, it would be easier if Nardone said he was taking it down for repairs rather than hauling it off.

Nardone got a friend with a large flatbed truck and they set out to retrieve the towering eagle. Just as the original owner's grandson had predicted, when Nardone and his helpers began taking it down with the help of a crane, a lot of people from town

In addition to "road art"—the many signs, gas pumps, and related automobilia he's collected—Nardone also likes street rods. This 1949 Chevy has a 454 under the hood and moves along very nicely. It's quite at home here among items that came from gas stations, drug stores, and diners doing business when the Chevy was new. *David Gooley*

stopped to ask what was happening. They all admired the sign and said they had been looking at it their whole lives. Rather than fib that he was just making repairs, Nardone told them he'd bought it and was there to haul it away. Yet he respected their devotion to it, so he offered to sell it to those who stopped and to the town. There were no takers. Everyone liked it but no one had room for it, and the town had no use for it either.

Though it's no longer in Nevada, the Richfield sign is now fully restored and affixed, as it should be, on the front of a service station. The only artifice is that it isn't a real, functioning station. But then, there are no operating Richfield stations, so Nardone's is as close as it gets. What made the sign worth all the effort was its condition. "The porcelain was perfect," Nardone says. Most of the neon lights were broken but there are shops around that can fix that. When they got the sign back to Nardone's house, they tested it and a little of the original neon still worked. He's had it all redone and now it looks as it did 70 years ago.

Against the backdrop of part of his vast sign collection are a few unusual pieces. He's had the fiberglass Ronald McDonald for about 25 years. They used to sit outside many of the restaurants around the country, but Nardo was told that children would often kiss them, raising hygiene concerns among parents. Ronald sits in a row of seats removed from a 1930s opera house in Seattle. Nardo bought the snowman new 15 years ago. When kids touch the snowman's arm, he moves and sings one of several Christmas carols. Everyone likes the snowman, and some people want one like it, but he's never seen another since he bought it. *David Gooley*

If your car runs out of gas, Nardo's Shell station unfortunately can't help you. But it can certainly refuel a person's pleasure in recalling the way service stations looked in a simpler time. This is not a real station relocated, but a reproduction Nardo created from his many years appreciating and photographing vanishing examples in small towns scattered around the country. *David Gooley*

Among the many passive objects he collects, Nardo also makes room for a few mobile ones. He's had this 1938 Chevy Delivery for 20 years. With an aluminum-head 350 Chevy crate engine under the hood, it definitely hauls. A decal on the rear side panel pertains to his wife's business, Nardo's Barber Shop. Surrounding the truck are many different "up-and-down" tire signs. Nardo likes this format because you can display a lot of them at once. *David Gooley*

In addition to his garages and memorabilia, Nardone also has a few street rods. "I can't drive more than one but I can look at a lot of them," he says. He's not rushing to expand those holdings though. "I have a big insurance bill," he laughs. It covers not only his cars but his memorabilia, which has been growing in value for decades.

While online marketplaces like eBay have made collecting easier, they're not for Nardone. "After two things, the thrill was gone," he admits. "I like to go out and find the stuff and hear the stories." What he had bought online were oil cans, of which he has a large collection, yet recovering them from a cardboard box sent by mail held no magic. Hearing that a can came from a small town is a lot less interesting than finding that boarded up store, talking with the owner, and venturing inside to find some castoffs that have lain hidden for decades. As with any other hobby, the hunt is often as rewarding as bagging the quarry itself.

Much of Nardone's stuff is emblazoned with "Nardo," a nickname a woman at a car show gave him years ago, simply by

Nardo appreciates his 1937 Chevy pickup but he feels a little guilty about it, too. He rarely drives it, in part because he doesn't fit in it very well. This bay also holds a sample of his auto battery signs. *David Gooley*

mispronouncing his real name. It stuck, and today, when he shows up at swap meets or car shows, that's the one he hears. It's also the name he's put on his "fake" service stations and his wife's (real) barber shop.

There's one service station item he's done collecting. "No more pumps," he declares. "I hurt my back moving those things around." Posterity won't suffer too much from this one limitation. He already has a wide selection and other folks have long since stepped in to buy, house and restore most any worthwhile ones that remain.

Nardone often welcomes visitors, though he doesn't care to book visits well in advance. "Car clubs want to get you into their calendar but I don't like to be tied down," he says. If a swap meet or car show pops up, he wants to be free to go. Without that liberty, the collection would never have gotten as large as it is today.

When strangers come to the gate, if they look like nice people, Nardo usually invites them for a look around. A couple from Holland recently appeared and he gave them a tour. "The man just loved it," Nardo says. "His wife liked it, too. He's a collector in Holland and he invited me to come and see his collection and to stay with them. His wife thanked me for making her husband's day."

The quaint reproduction Richfield station has an inviting look—like an old cabin. The sign out front is a modest example, though the company made some that were much more impressive. *David Gooley*

Index